Much to do
about
Education

Anne Corbett is a journalist, at present living in France from where she writes for *New Society* and other journals. She is a former education correspondent of *New Society*, a one time regular contributor to the *Times Educational Supplement* and the author of the Fabian Society evidence to the Taylor Committee on government and management of schools (*Whose Schools?* published in 1976). She also has written for courses run by the Open University's Faculty of Educational Studies. She was chairman of a working party of the Library Advisory Council (England) which produced a report in the Department of Education and Science's Library Information Series (*The Libraries' Choice*, published by HMSO).

She is married with two sons.

Much to do about Education

4th edition

Anne Corbett

Published for the Council for
Educational Advance by

M

Macmillan Education

First published by the Council for
Educational Advance 1968
Reprinted 1968 (eight times), 1969
Second edition 1969
Reprinted 1970 (twice), 1971, 1972
Third edition 1973
This fourth edition published for
the Council for Educational Advance
by Macmillan Education 1978

MACMILLAN EDUCATION LIMITED
Houndmills Basingstoke Hampshire RG21 2XS
and London
Associated companies in Delhi Dublin
Hong Kong Johannesburg Lagos Melbourne
New York Singapore and Tokyo

Printed in Great Britain by A. Wheaton & Co. Ltd., Exeter

CONTENTS

Introduction   vii

15 to 18   1
The Crowther Report

Half our Future   8
The Newsom Report

Higher Education   13
The Robbins Report

Children and their Primary Schools   23
The Plowden Report

Public Schools Commission   34
The Newsom and Donnison Reports

Teacher Education and Training   45
The James Report

Adult Education: A Plan for Development   52
The Russell Report

A Language for Life   58
The Bullock Report

A New Partnership for Our Schools   63
The Taylor Report

ACKNOWLEDGEMENTS

My thanks are due to the efficient and willing staff of the National Union of Teacher's library, who lightened the task of revising this edition.

Anne Corbett

INTRODUCTION

This survey deals with the expectations and fate of the major educational reports published in the last twenty years. They are part of a tradition which goes back to the early nineteenth century when the difficult issues for government were how to finance the education of 'the lower classes in the metropolis and beyond,' and its responsibilities to church schools and pupil teachers. In the 150 years since, educational committees of enquiry have dealt with nearly every important contemporary issue[1].

The reports considered here start with reviews of secondary education, which the 1944 Education Act made universal (Crowther and Newsom), the consequential demand for more higher education (Robbins), the state of primary education (Plowden), and a perennial issue, the future of the 'public' schools (Newsom again and Donnison). Plowden marked a turning point. After that there was a more limited review of adult education (Russell) and the establishment of a committee on special education (Warnock) whose work proved so wide-ranging that its work seemed endlessly blocked. The other reports in this survey are concerned with particular questions: the reorganisation of teacher training (James), standards of reading and the use of language (Bullock) and the government of schools (Taylor).

Most of the early reports are products of the Central Advisory Council for Education which the 1944 act required ministers to set up. But despite the statutory requirement, the council has been dormant since Plowden finished work, justified by governments in the light of a declining economy, and their continuing concern to avoid the reviews which might substantially increase public expenditure. All the reports published since 1970 are from *ad hoc* committees whose success has quite largely depended on whether they have been able to act like a central advisory council, or at least draw on similar resources.

It is the argument of this survey that, whatever the state of the economy, the English education system needs its major reviews. The committees of enquiry have occupied a place which no other body seems able to fill. Relatively free from the day to day pressures of government, local education authorities and inspectorate, they have been much the best placed to stimulate the long-term thinking without which reform is shakily based. Theirs has been a unique forum for airing questions, clarifying options and proposing policies. They have created the context in which it has been

[1] For the historical record, see J. Stuart Maclure, *Educational Documents, England and Wales, 1816 to the present*, Methuen, 1975

possible to evaluate government response. The evidence they have inspired, the research most of them have commissioned, has proved a fertile ground for other work; if not altogether in the spirit of Karl Marx working his way through the nineteenth century reports on social reform in the reading room of the British Museum. These reports create their own Before Christ-Anno Domini time scale: a reference point for policy.

Undoubtedly the committees have weaknesses. They are generally slow to reach conclusions, laboured in style. One permanent secretary at the Department of Education and Science even went on record as saying that they were 'an entire waste of words and a waste of time'.[2] They tend to be trapped in the conventions of a middle-aged, middle class membership, too tied to the system to indulge in strong criticism or controversy.

This survey includes the sad story of the Public Schools Commissions, from whom ministers longed for practical advice, reports which would have been implemented to the last dotted 'i' and crossed 't' if only the committees could have agreed. There are other parallels. No committee of the relevant period was prepared to consider comprehensive reorganisation, the major educational issue of the late 1950s and 1960s. None looked directly at the way reorganisation was working out.

Nevertheless it was this kind of committee which changed the political climate of thinking about nursery and primary education, higher education and teacher training. Their insistence on monitoring made it politically possible for the government to assume some responsibility for educational standards. Their reports, tracing the failure of the 1944 Act to provide educational equality, gave authority for radical reform. Starting with proposals confined to the education system, such as the urgent need to raise the school leaving age, they moved within ten years to arguing that education policy should be directed to doing everything possible to counter social and economic disadvantage: Plowden's proposal for educational priority areas.

Many of their proposals have not been implemented. The following pages record examples of changes promised in principle but largely ignored in practice, such as the reform of the teacher's probationary year and the introduction of universal in-service training. They also show reforms taken up, like nursery education, but only on a token scale. Other proposals, apparently adopted, were trimmed in the light of later developments: that, for example, includes the commitment to providing higher education places in the 1980s for all the able and willing. But there is an achievement, too,

[2] Sir Herbert Andrew, quoted in Maurice Kogan and Tim Packwood, Advisory Councils and Committees in Education, Routledge and Kegan Paul, 1974

in leaving much to do on the educational agenda. The arguments and evidence are there to be used by later campaigners.

The committees' most distinctive legacy has been their concern with quality. It is easy to deride some sometimes fatuous statements. But there are not any effective alternatives. Perhaps because the system is decentralised and the secretary of state has no very clear role on curriculum, there is no other obvious forum for discussing aims and achievements. The deficiency is the more marked when the main political issues are quantitative: and the logistics of manpower and resources have dominated much of the last decade. In that period Newsom and Plowden have showed up the inadequacies of mass education in ways to which governments had to respond. Bullock applied a similarly effective analysis across part of the school curriculum. But since then there has been nothing similar.

Another way of measuring the committees' achievements is to note what happened in their absence. It seems no accident that the worst gaps in provision and thinking have been where they were most marginally involved. Further education was only a subsidiary theme of the 1959 Crowther report and has not been considered since. As youth unemployment started to rise in the 1970s, there were no resources within the education system from which to conjure reform: the external and generously-financed Manpower Services Commission had to be brought in to the rescue.

There is a more striking, and possibly more damaging example in the activity which followed the 1976 speech of the prime minister, James Callaghan, on a variety of educational arguments: the curriculum and standards, the links between school and employment, and the education and training of teachers. In a period in which educational issues had become uncharacteristically partisan, a way had to be found of turning controversy into consensus. Central advisory councils, dormant ten years, clearly could not respond quickly. *Ad hoc* committees had had variable fates. The Department of Education and Science was by then better organised than it had been a decade previously to do some reviewing of its own: the HM Inspectorate was working more on surveys, less on advising and inspecting small groups of teachers or schools. The department had its own units on the assessment of performance and educational disadvantage. The Secretary of State, Mrs Shirley Williams, decided to take on almost single-handed with the DES, the job of drawing reform out of national debate. There was scarcely time for the diffusely-structured education world to produce considered opinions, no time at all to put them in any perspective. The government had already produced a 'Green' discussion paper, *Education in Schools: A Consultative Document*.

It looked in 1977 as if it would enable the government to produce some sort of policy document as a result to show that it cared about standards too. But it was a curious, and possibly foolish, way of treating the local authorities and teachers who have to make the system work. Deprived of the debate and self-education which goes on while committees are sitting and when their recommendations are published, they are immediately less involved in the change that the government wants. It is a classic way of widening the centre-grass roots gap. It is also tempting to suggest that had the government been less concerned to avoid wide-ranging reviews, the 1970s controversies might themselves have been less bitter.

Ironically, the expense which governments so dreaded incurring, has not determined the eventual fate of reports. Although the immediate reaction to reports was often conditioned by the luck of the economic draw, their success in the end depended on how well their reforms could be fitted into the system. Plowden proposals were still being implemented ten years after publication. Crowther, Robbins and James all provided a base on which much else could be built. The effective reports were clearly free of the rigours of political time-tables.

What, then, of the future? On the evidence of recent educational history, the government should be looking up the Education Act, 1944, section 4, which begins:

> There shall be two central advisory councils for education, one for England, the other for Wales and Monmouthshire, and it shall be the duty of those councils to advise the Secretary of State upon such matters connected with educational theory and practice as they think fit, and upon any questions referred to them by him....

It should be working out ways of enabling the councils to work more quickly by improving some of the existing sources of data, and how it might be more adventurous about membership. The government should not be allowed to let the matter slip.

For there has been no sign during the recent period that the committees' essential virtue has been replaced: their unique capacity to create a consensus for change. In a system which takes a lot to shift, that is the most stable base for development that any government has.

---

report of the Central Advisory Council (England)
vol I   1959 HMSO   62½p
vol II   1960 HMSO   50p

Chairman: Sir Geoffrey Crowther
Members: Mr G. S. Bosworth, Mr M. H. Brown, Mr M. H. Cadbury,
Ald. S. M. Caffyn, Mr A. B. Clegg, Dr H. Frazer, Mr T. F. Gilbert, Miss B. A.
Godwin, Miss M. G. Green, Dr V. M. Grubb, Dr R. Holroyd, Miss E. M.
Hoxstep, Lord James of Rusholme, Miss A. P. Jephcott, Prof. A. V. Judges,
Mr B. G. Lampard-Vachell, Sir Patrick Linstead, Prof. N. F. Mott, Mr W. F.
Oakeshott, Mr S. H. Porter, Prof. S. G. Raybould, Dr M. E. Reeves,
Prof. T. S. Simey, Mr G. H. Sylvester, Dr P. F. R. Venables, Mr H. A. Warren,
Miss E. M. Wedekind, Mr J. V. C. Wray, Mr B. W. M. Young *plus* Miss C.
Avent (co-opted), Lt Gen. Sir Kenneth McLean and Mr O. W. Mitchell (who
both resigned) and Dr J. Macalister Brew (deceased).
Assessor: Mr D. G. O. Ayerst, HMI.
Secretary: Mr J. A. Humphreys.

Terms of reference: To consider, in relation to the changing social and
industrial needs of our society, and the needs of its individual citizens, the
education of boys and girls between the ages of 15 and 18; and, in
particular, to consider the balance at various levels of general and
specialised studies, and to examine the interrelationship of the various
stages of education.

With Crowther, the Central Advisory Council was given for the first time in
the ten years or so of its life, terms of reference which could tap the roots
of the English education system. It had to consider how to implement the
1944 Act's clauses on raising the school leaving age to sixteen and
establishing county colleges for part-time education up to the age of
eighteen: a brief which invited some assessment of secondary progress in
general since the Act.

With Crowther, the Central Advisory Council for the first time produced
a report to rival those of the pre-war Consultative Committees such as
those chaired by Sir William Hadow. Crowther also began the Central
Advisory Council tradition of research which was to make an important
contribution to educational sociology during the 1960s. Its national service
survey, in particular, produced much new information on the relationship
between ability, school career and school and family characteristics.

Many of the Crowther recommendations were curricular, and hence the concern of schools and colleges not the government. These set the tone for the whole report, which was dominated by its thinking on the sixth form. It has been called the last great defence of intellectual discipleship, because though it considered pupils should take fewer A levels and spend more time on general education, it was essentially a defence of an elitist sixth-form tradition.

Associated with this thinking was the commitment to a tripartite system of secondary education. Crowther would even have extended it into further education, with a highly individual interpretation of the county college idea as put forward in the Fisher Act of 1918, and then in the 1944 Act. Crowther saw county colleges as 'an alternative road' for the non-academic. The tripartite philosophy dominated, too, the ideas about teachers, beyond Crowther's direct terms of reference. Crowther wanted more preferential treatment for graduates and secondary schools teachers on the continental model. 'Teachers are not a homogeneous body and will become less so with the growth to the upper forms of schools.' This was not popular with the associations representing the vast majority of teachers, who had only just won the abolition of secondary and elementary codes, under the 1944 Act.

If support for tripartism had been Crowther's sole theme, the report might well have been forgotten. By 1959 a strictly stratified secondary system had many opponents. But Crowther had another theme – and had a more receptive audience for it. It created a national awareness of the waste in elitist higher education and an out-of-date and haphazard approach to industrial training. It linked this with arguments for social justice.

The council recommended the almost immediate raising of the school leaving age, measures to encourage sixth formers from poorer homes, the introduction of county colleges and the reorganisation of industrial training, in pursuit of its twin aims: 'the right of every boy and girl to be educated' and 'the need of the community to provide an adequate supply of brains and skill to sustain its economic activity.' The problem, as the council saw it, was that 'even in the education of our brightest children – which is what the English system does best – there is still a grave waste of talent through too early an abandonment of formal education. We do not think that the figure of twelve per cent of the age group still in full-time education at the age of seventeen and of six per cent at twenty is nearly good enough. The education that is provided for the great mass of children is inadequate both in its quality and its duration. In the middle, between the brightest quarter and the great mass of ordinary children the deficiencies relative to the need are greatest of all; for it is in this second quartile that the richest vein of untapped human resources lies, which will have to be exploited if this country is to keep a place among the nations that are in the van of spiritual and material progress.'

Main recommendations

Secondary Modern Schools
Extended courses should be available – ultimately for all fifteen year olds but by 1965 for half of them. Where possible these courses should be in schools attended by pupils since the age of eleven. Pupils in the lower half of the modern school range should have local or regional leaving certificates: external exams should be avoided because of their warping effect on the curriculum, unless they too are locally or regionally based.

Secondary education for all
The minimum school leaving age should be raised to sixteen in one of the academic years between 1966-7 and 1968-9. As an interim measure there should be two instead of three leaving dates during the school year.

County colleges
There should be compulsory part-time education in county colleges for those up to the age of eighteen not going on to full-time further or higher education, and a strengthened youth service as an essential complement to county colleges. Potential county college students should immediately be encouraged to do day-release. After the school leaving age had been raised, county college attendance (in purpose-built premises) should be compulsory in one or two areas, becoming gradually compulsory region by region.

The sixth form
More attention should be paid to broadening the basis of the curriculum in the fourth and fifth years of secondary school, and to preventing four-fifths of pupils choosing a specialisation by the age of thirteen or fourteen. More should be done to attract teachers with first-class degrees into teaching. The tradition of sixth form specialisation should be maintained, but measures should be taken to counteract its most narrowing effects. More university places were urgently needed, especially for girls. But a speedy and uniform system for dealing with all university applications would immediately reduce some of the frustrations; as would the recognition that GCE A level was primarily a school examination. It should be used as a qualification for university entrance but in no circumstances should A level marks provide the means of selection. Pupils should not take more than three GCE A levels. The design of minority subjects should be improved and should include common and complementary elements to make science

3

specialists more literate, arts specialists more numerate. (The word numeracy was made fashionable by the Crowther committee.)

Local education authorities should be able to offer substantial eighth year bursaries to enable three years to be spent in the sixth form by pupils who would otherwise have left.

Further education

Half the sixteen to eighteen year olds should be in full-time education by 1979 (in contrast to the twelve per cent or so in 1959) since they were basically the technicians and craftsmen of the future.

The long-term aim should be a coherent national system of practical education instead of the current patchwork – there should be more consistent provision across further education colleges for technician, craftsman and operative grades; a closer relationship between apprenticeship and further education; more day-release opportunities for girls; less dependence on evening classes. Block release should be used wherever possible.

Until the raising of the school-leaving age there should be one-year full-time introductory courses in technical colleges for boys finding it difficult to obtain apprenticeships with day release. The 'alternative road' for non-academic pupils could be provided in schools or in colleges of further education and the practical approach envisaged should not be confined to technical subjects.

Institutions and teachers

There should be a choice of institutions – by age-range, sex and provision for part-time and full-time courses.

Provision should be made in further education colleges for academic courses parallel to school sixth forms. Practical courses could be provided in either schools or colleges. There should be more secondary technical schools and these should have disproportionately large sixth forms to allow for transfers. Comprehensive schools could be introduced in certain circumstances, e.g., where there is already a variety of schools or in thinly populated areas.

More teachers would be needed. With the raising of the school-leaving age the teacher-pupil ratio in secondary schools should not be allowed to fall below 1:17 or 1:19. The National Advisory Council for the Training and Supply of Teachers should be asked to advise on the extra numbers for raising the school-leaving age and on ways of improving the supply of college trained teachers. Efforts should also be made to attract more graduates: salaries should compare with other professions open to graduates. Married women should be encouraged to return. Teachers should be given more clerical help. There should be greater variety in the

4

conditions of employment to encourage the recruitment of university graduates to sixth forms and county colleges.

In those areas which suffer from a shortage of teachers or a high rate of turnover there should be experiments with salary increments or housing for teachers to try and reverse such trends.

A plan
These proposals should be adopted as a coherent properly-phased programme for the twenty years up to 1980 and not left to the mercies of the parliamentary time-table and the economic situation.

Action on the report

The Crowther report suffered two misfortunes. It reported just after an election, when there was little incentive to do anything about it. Worse, it was wrong in its basic premise that in the 1960s the number of teachers would expand just as the numbers of pupils would fall. By 1959 it was clear that the birth-rate was continuing to rise. There were not going to be the extra teachers to make raising the school-leaving age easy.

The Conservative government, in its period of office up to 1964, agreed to relatively minor changes which were implemented by the 1962 Education Act. It agreed to the Crowther recommendation of abolishing the Christmas leaving date; but it needed ten years' lobbying to get a firm commitment to raising the minimum leaving age to sixteen (see page 11). It also agreed to some improvements in university grants, but would not do anything about grants for sixth formers. The government's other step was to set in train work which eventually produced some important results. It established a commission under Lord Robbins' chairmanship to examine higher education and to investigate the sixth form crisis (see page 13). It also established a working party under the chairmanship of Mr Robert Beloe to decide on the structure of an examination which eventually became the Certificate of Secondary Education.

Crowther had been anxious to ensure that the curriculum which most pupils followed should not be distorted by the examination needs of a few. 'The majority ought not to be subjected to an external examination and their interests must be protected.' A teacher-controlled examination, however, might be a way of meeting an important minority need, perhaps of a third of secondary modern pupils. In practice, the Certificate of Secondary Education has proved to be infinitely flexible: subject-based, organised in a number of ways to give teachers the degree of participation they wish, and spanning a range of marks within the reach of almost all pupils up to the equivalent of GCE O level. Once a five-year secondary

5

school course became compulsory with the raising of the school-leaving age, four-fifths of all school leavers gained at least one CSE subject pass or better.

Its success led the Schools Council in the late 1960s to propose a similar type of examination for older candidates, including those in further education. This, the Certificate of Extended Education, had been run on an experimental basis since 1974, awaiting full approval from the Secretary of State.

Sixth form curricula, for those wanting to go on to higher education, proved much more intractable. Ever since the Schools Council was set up in 1964 with a responsibility to advise the Secretary of State on examinations policy, the sixth form has been on the agenda. There have been a number of attempts at reform, chiefly in the Crowther style of broadening the subject base. Further proposals for a five subject approach (N and F: Normal and Further) were due to be published in 1978.

Similarly, other Crowther recommendations were taken up years later. The 1944 Act had said little about further education. But by the 1950s it was clear that it was an important – and expensive – responsibility of the local education authorities. During the 1960s a pattern was gradually established along the lines the Crowther report suggested: a majority of colleges provided technician courses up to the age of eighteen, regional colleges provided for more advanced work, and the colleges of advanced technology, later to become universities (see page 16), provided degree-level work. The incentive to keep industrial education and training up-to-date did not become pressing until even later: in 1973, the Technician Education Council and the Business Educational Council were established to assess standards and award diplomas. By 1977–8 over 40 000 students were registered for their courses.

There were some gaps criticised by Crowther that have never been filled. Large numbers of young people have never had any access to further education after leaving school, although there is ample evidence that some early school leavers turn avidly to education later. There was no move to establish compulsory part-time education in the county colleges. The Industrial Training Act, 1964, dealt only with provision for those whose job clearly demanded some training. Yet, even as late as 1977 almost half a year's school leavers (300 000 or so) were going into jobs where release for further education was seldom granted. Only the terrible reality of youth unemployment forced a change in policy. In 1977, the government agreed to a recommendation of the recently-created Manpower Services Commission to establish a programme of combined training and work experience for 230 000 young unemployed between the ages of sixteen and eighteen, to start fully in September 1978.

The economic crisis also gave fresh life to another Crowther theme: the need to plan. Not that the approach succeeded. The ten-year strategy enunciated in the 1972 White Paper, *Education: a Framework for Expansion* was swiftly cut back in the face of further crises.

The question of grants for sixth-formers has also been revived. In response to a recommendation from a House of Commons Expenditure committee, the government started to look at the question again in 1974, making it clear that no action could be contemplated immediately.

HALF OUR FUTURE

report of the Central Advisory Council (England)
1963 HMSO   52½p

Chairman: Mr John Newsom
Members: Mr R. H. Adams, Miss C. Avent, Mr D. B. Bartlett, Mr S. W.
Buglass, Ald. S. M. Caffyn, Mr A. B. Clegg, Prof. B. A. Fletcher, Mr F. D.
Flower, Dr H. Frazer, Mr A. J. N. Fuller, Miss M. G. Green, Rev. H. W. Hinds,
Mrs A. J. Hirst, Mr R. M. T. Kneebone, Dr K. Ollerenshaw, Miss B. Paston
Brown, Miss E. L. Sewell, Miss A. M. Simcock, Mr W. J. Slater, Mr J. E. Smith,
Mr C. A. Thompson, Mr N. G. Treloar, Mr D. Winnard *plus* Lord Amory,
Dame Anne Godwin and Miss N. Newton Smith (all resigned).
Assessors: Miss K. A. Kennedy; Mr D. G. O. Ayerst, HMI; Mr R. J. W.
Stubbings, HMI; Mr J. W. Withrington, HMI.
Secretary: Miss M. J. Marshall, HMI.

Terms of reference: To consider the education between the ages of
thirteen and sixteen of pupils of average or less than average ability who
are, or will be, following full-time courses, either at schools or in establish-
ments of further education. The term education shall be understood to
include extra curricular activities.

Having covered some of the same ground as Crowther and drawn on some
of the same material, Newsom came to basically the same conclusion: that
the world is divided between a top, middle and bottom. But, reinforced by
a survey which looked at the facilities available to the bright (the Browns
of the survey) the middle (the Jones) and the bottom (the Robinsons),
Newsom went on to argue that some of these resources should be
redistributed.

Basically 'Newsom' pupils 'constitute approximately half the pupils in
our secondary schools: they will eventually become half the citizens of this
country, half the workers; half the mothers and fathers, and half the
consumers. . . . They should be entitled to half of the best that the system
could give them.'

A fine ideal: yet curiously Newsom avoided one of the relevant issues.
Setting up the enquiry implied concern with, if not the failure of, the
secondary modern idea. The committee scarcely questioned whether a
divided school system, which selected a bright minority through the eleven
plus, and labelled the rest as failures, could in itself be responsible for some
of the problems.

The remedy as the committee saw it, lay not in organisational change to comprehensive schooling, but in a change of attitude 'among the policy makers and the public at large.' Why should being a Robinson, or even a Jones, mean worse buildings, teachers and courses? Newsom showed that twenty per cent of schools served problem areas and were attended by eighteen per cent of all secondary pupils. About seven per cent of the schools were in run-down urban areas, but a further thirteen per cent shared some of their disadvantages. Whereas forty per cent of the council's modern school sample had seriously inadequate buildings – a shaming enough figure – the corresponding figure for schools in slums was seventy-nine per cent. Only a third of the women teachers and half the men had been on the staff more than three years. School work for pupils in their schools was likely to be highly traditional and much resented. Also, deprivations at school were more often than not paralleled by deprivation at home.

Reform therefore required some improvement in physical conditions. It also implied tackling the point put by a pupil: 'The school could all be marble, sir, but it would still be a bloody school.' The whole style of school work needed reform. Instead of a watered-down grammar school curriculum, these pupils should have something in their own right: 'more realistic and adult.'

Main recommendations

The pupils and the schools
An immediate announcement should be made that the school-leaving age would be raised to sixteen for all pupils entering secondary schools from September 1965.

The Department of Education should institute a research programme into techniques of teaching pupils whose abilities are artificially depressed by environmental and linguistic handicaps. An interdepartmental working party should be set up to deal with the general social and educational problems of slum areas.

Curricula and exams
All schools should be able to provide a choice of fourth and fifth year courses for which pupils should not be rigidly streamed. The more that such courses are given 'a realistic and adult reference' the better. The final-year school programme should be deliberately outgoing and links with the youth employment service, further education, the youth service and adult education strengthened. 'Work experience' courses might be appropriate.

Teachers should recognise and make use of major out-of-school influences on their pupils' lives, such as television and Saturday jobs.

All school leavers should be given a leaving certificate, irrespective of whether they have taken public examinations. Schools should not pressure unsuitable pupils into taking public examinations.

Local education authorities should consider revising the agreed syllabus for religious education to make it more suitable for older pupils. Schools should give positive guidance on sexual behaviour.

Pupils should spend more time on educational, including extra-curricular, activities. All should have homework. Staffing implications of a longer school day would need to be examined. Some of the work might be done by joint teacher-youth leaders.

The Department of Education and the LEAs should undertake a survey of provision for residential courses and should estimate the cost of providing some residential experience for all pupils during the course of their school life.

Buildings

The Department of Education and LEAs should arrange an experimental building programme to try out different forms of school organisation and teaching methods.

The secondary modern schools in slums should be replaced, and over-crowded but otherwise adequate modern schools should be extended.

There should be more provision for practical subjects, possibly in conjunction with further education colleges. Secondary schools should be provided with audio-visual aids, and account taken at the planning stage of the possibility of providing television and language teaching equipment for new buildings.

Teachers

A substantial proportion of secondary school teachers should have con-current training (the usual pattern for college of education three-year courses, as opposed to the university one-year training, following after the degree studies). Colleges should train teachers for 'Newsom' pupils, to teach in one main and one (preferably two) other subjects. Training should immediately start to include preparation for raising the school-leaving age.

Training should become compulsory for graduates from a date to be announced. As an interim measure there should be emergency in-service courses for qualified, but untrained, teachers.

Action on the report

Sir Edward Boyle, the Conservative minister who received the Newsom report, implicitly strengthened its message: 'The essential point,' he wrote in the foreword, 'is that all children should have an equal opportunity of acquiring intelligence and developing their talents and abilities to the full.' But the Conservative government was out of office before it had time to consider the implications of how to translate that into practice. Nor did the Labour government take it up, at least not until after the Plowden committee worked out a strategy for positive discrimination four years later (see page 24).

The Conservative government accepted in 1964 that the school-leaving age should be raised to sixteen. It was not to be in 1969-70 as the council suggested, but in 1970-71, when there would still be relatively small age-groups moving through the secondary schools.

In 1968, the Labour government, faced with the need to cut back public expenditure postponed the reform till 1972-3, as a means of immediately saving the 100 million pounds which had been allocated for 'RSLA' building. It was left to another Conservative minister (Mrs Margaret Thatcher in 1971) to approve the crucial building programmes to enable the extra pupils to stay on.

Not only did the 'Newsom' children have to wait longer for a better deal Ironically the Labour government thereby seriously damaged its own policies. The RSLA building programmes were being used by almost all local education authorities to further local secondary reorganisation. The loss of such funds set back the comprehensive policy by several years, since it was not an object the subsequent Conservative government wished to pursue: it went so far as to ensure that the secondary building programmes were among the smallest ever.

RSLA when it came had a relatively bad press. Much of the initial public comment focused on the misbehaviour and truancy of some of the 'conscripts'. But the view of the Department of Education, shared by most local education authority opinion, was that schools had sufficient materials, equipment and accommodation to implement the change. 'A great deal of encouraging and imaginative work' was being done by teachers, reported the HM Inspectorate one year later: experience 'is by and large encouraging.'

This was fairly remarkable, given the economic setbacks, the hazards of curriculum reform in a decentralised system and the fact that outside London, local authorities were simultaneously caught up in a reorganisation of local government. But there was much evidence of the enormous efforts made by teachers and local education authorities.

RSLA had been a natural priority for the Schools Council, set up in 1964 to encourage curriculum development and coordinate examination policy. Its working papers and development projects provided the initial stimulus in many authorities and schools to new courses. The 450 or so teachers' centres became a focus for local teacher training and discussion. Some authorities and some schools launched out on their own, sticking to the tradition that since responsibility for the content and method of teaching lies at local level, much of the initiative ought to come from there too.

The result was a vast number of new courses, many with a 'Newsom' sound. They ranged from learning about the analysis and production of cosmetics to studying personal relationships: distinctly different from those provided for academic pupils. There was also some enthusiasm for community service courses for the new school leavers. But it was soon clear that the real expansion was in examination courses. The flexibility of the Certificate of Secondary Education has been mentioned (see page 5). For most schools, examination courses provided welcome structures and aims which were much more difficult to develop in the non-examination courses which Crowther and Newsom would have liked to see. A number of authorities also developed – often with difficulty – linked courses with further education colleges, to give pupils some experience of the sort of trade courses which were not necessarily available at school, such as bricklaying and plumbing. However, work-experience courses, advocated by Newsom, turned out to be full of problems with unions and employers, even after amending legislation in 1973 and DES guidance in 1974.

It was a measure of how quickly assumptions changed, that the HM Inspectors ended their 1975 report by suggesting that there was a danger in identifying 'standardised' RSLA or Newsom pupils. A more subtle interpretation was needed of 'equal but realistic opportunities.'

One reason, of course, was that school rejection remained a problem. The DES continued to assert that misbehaviour, especially violent misbehaviour, was not widespread. But a number of schools in Britain, as indeed elsewhere, had their task made more difficult by longer compulsory schooling. The Labour government's Education Act, 1976, dealt with the most prominent form of truancy by abolishing it: they moved the leaving date to immediately after examinations.

On the rather more solid ground of the education of teachers, Newsom proved a sounder guide. Many of its recommendations on teacher training were eventually taken up again by the James enquiry (see page 45) set up by the 1970 Conservative government. It was also agreed that graduate teachers should in future have to have some training. This became compulsory in primary schools from 1970, in secondary schools from 1974, for all but mathematics and science teachers who were in short supply.

HIGHER EDUCATION

report of the committee appointed by the Prime Minister
report 1963   Cmnd 2154   HMSO   £1.20

appendix one   The demand for places in higher education 1963
Cmnd 2154-I   HMSO   90p

appendix two   Students and their education (two volumes) 1964
Cmnd 2154-II-I   HMSO   £1.00
Cmnd 2154-II-II   HMSO   £1.37½

appendix three   Teachers in higher education 1963
Cmnd 2154-III   HMSO   75p

appendix four   Administrative, financial and economic aspects of higher education 1963
Cmnd 2154-IV   HMSO   62½p

appendix five   Higher education in other countries 1964
Cmnd 2154-V   HMSO   90p

Chairman: Lord Robbins
Members: Sir David Anderson, Dame Kitty Anderson, Mr A. Chenevix-Trench, Prof. J. Drever, Mr H. L. Elvin, Miss H. L. Gardner, Sir Patrick Linstead, Sir Philip Morris, Mr H. C. Shearman, Mr R. B. Southall and Sir Edward Herbert (deceased).
Treasury: Mr P. S. Ross (secretary).

Terms of reference: To review the pattern of full-time higher education in Great Britain, and, in the light of national resources, to advise HM Government on what principles its long-term development should be based. In particular, to advise whether there should be any changes in that pattern, whether any new types of institution are desirable and whether any modifications should be made in the present arrangements for planning and co-ordinating the various types of institution.

The Robbins report gets bracketed with the other major educational reports of the last ten years. But it was very different in kind. In the first place, it was a politically important document. Having been set up by a prime minister (Mr Harold Macmillan), it reported in an immediately pre-election period. These two facts almost assured it of success. It was also well placed for civil service politics, with a Treasury man as secretary. Indeed, in stark contrast to the Central Advisory Council reports, a full government statement was issued within twenty-four hours of publication, accepting many of the main recommendations. Most staggering contrast of all was the commitment to the report's ten-year programme – and to its £3500 million cost. Secondly, Robbins was not, like the Central Advisory Councils, concerned with the curricular content of its sector of the system. Its sole concern was structure. The report was a programme for action.

Its achievement was to revolutionise thinking about the scale of higher education. It became accepted that there would have to be an increase in places between 1970 and 1980 at least as large as the entire higher education provision in 1962 (over 200 000), a calculation deriving from Robbins' premise that there should be higher education places for all who were qualified and wanted it. Robbins effectively exploded the notion that only a small and fixed proportion of the population was fit to receive higher education.

Associated with this principle of providing for the able and willing was the Robbins conviction that there should be equal academic awards for equal academic performance, since what was being recognised was the individual's achievement. In other words, students taking degree-level courses outside universities should be able to get degrees - not just 'degree level' qualifications. The committee was also strongly in favour of wide opportunities for transfer between institutions.

The other great Robbins contribution was to stimulate a design for higher education which brought the universities for the first time firmly into the sphere of public responsibility. Before Robbins, there were the same three sets of institutions providing higher education: universities, colleges of further education and teacher-training colleges. The universities remained separate from the rest of the education system, both individually and collectively – a separation emphasised by the fact that their channel of communication with the government, the University Grants Committee, received its money from the Treasury, not the Ministry of Education.

That had been reasonable enough in the 1920s, when although the universities accepted state aid, it had been only £1 million or so a year. It was only £4 million in the 1940s. By the late 1970s the government was meeting over seventy per cent of recurrent and ninety per cent of capital costs – £317 million a year in 1973–4 – almost £1 million a day. There was an educational case, too, for bringing universities into closer contact with schools in the maintained sector, as demand for higher education grew.

The further education and teacher-training colleges, firmly in local education authority control, had benefitted from important developments before Robbins, which had raised their status fairly effectively. The teacher-training course had been lengthened from two to three years in 1960, and a target set for expansion to 80 000 students by 1970. The 1956 White Paper, *Technical Education*, introduced some system into the technical college field, designating a hierarchy of colleges with ten colleges of advanced technology at the top. This reform was continued by the White Paper, *Better Opportunities in Technical Education* (1961), which set out a policy for rationalising courses between institutions.

The Robbins report was accompanied by the most sophisticated statistics ever used in an educational report. These ran to five appendices. Special surveys were undertaken for the report at a cost of £45 000. They provided much important evidence on the pool of ability, the unquestionable demand for higher education, the low level of university provision by comparison with other countries, and the comparatively widespread degree-level provision outside universities.

Main recommendations

Places
Places should be provided for 390 000 full-time students in 1973–4 and for 560 000 in 1980–81 (compared with 216 000 in 1962–3). This would increase the proportion of the age group from eight to seventeen per cent by 1980, without relaxing the degree of competition for entry.

School/higher education links
There should be more effective links between schools and higher education. Oxbridge dominance should be counteracted by generous capital grants to other universities. The Universities Central Council on Admissions should cover all universities and the colleges of advanced technology. There should be research by an independent body into the extent aptitude tests might supplement other features of the selection process (e.g. GCE A levels and interviews).

Style and structure of higher education
It was essential that universities should provide more broadly-based first-degree courses in the three year period (as in Scotland). Highly specialised degree courses were irrelevant for most students and damaging for the schools. The proportion of postgraduates should increase from twenty to thirty per cent; there should be a more generous system of postgraduate awards and more supervision of postgraduate work.

Great changes should be made in the structure of teacher training. Nearly all colleges should grow to more than 750 students. As well as the three-year concurrent courses of simultaneous education and training, there should be four-year courses in the training colleges leading to a professional qualification and degree. Training colleges should be renamed colleges of education, to reflect their wider purpose. Colleges within each university's institute of education and the university's department of education should be formed into a school of education. Each school should be responsible to the university senate for the degrees awarded to the college of education students. Colleges should have independent governing bodies. Colleges should be financed by earmarked grants from a grants commission.

There should be a number of changes in the system of further education and an expansion in the provision of technological education. This should include an expansion in postgraduate technological work. Five institutions, to be known as Special Institutions for Scientific and Technological Education and Research (SISTERs), should be selected for the development of high level work. Colleges of Advanced Technology (CAT) should be designated technological universities, with power to award higher as well as first degrees and their financing should be transferred to the Grants Commission. Two Scottish Central Institutions should follow the same path. The others should be linked with Strathclyde (Technological) University or should operate like English regional colleges. These latter should develop a wider range of studies; most should continue to be maintained by local education authorities, though some might federate with another technical or training college to become universities.

Area and commercial colleges should continue to be locally-based and only those likely to be selected for regional college status should provide for advanced work. Students on approved degree-level courses in the further education sector should be able to work for honours, pass and higher degrees. These should be awarded by a Council for National Academic Awards. There should be legislation to prevent unauthorised bodies from awarding degrees.

For art education, the Royal College of Art should be treated administratively like the colleges of advanced technology and brought within the Grants Commission ambit. Advanced work in art colleges should lead to the already established Diploma in Art and Design, rather than degrees.

The College of Aeronautics should also come into the Grants Commission sphere, and should probably link up with a university.

Future pattern of higher education
The recommended expansion of higher education should be possible within the existing range of institutions. Future planning should cover a period ten years ahead and estimates should be provided for that time.

Universities should provide 350 000 of the 560 000 places needed in higher education by 1980-81: this would bring their share of higher education places up from fifty-five per cent in 1962 to sixty per cent in 1980. About 300 000 of the university places might be provided in existing universities (including the CATs) especially if they were expanded to the Oxbridge size of 8000-10 000 students. A further 30 000 places should be provided in six new universities, which should be sited in or near large centres of population, and 20 000 places in some ten regional colleges, Scottish central institutions and colleges of education which had attained university status, either in their own right or in conjunction with existing universities.

Colleges of education should provide 145 000 places for prospective teachers in 1980-81. They should also cater increasingly for non-teachers. At the same date, there should be 65 000 places for full-time advanced students in further education.

The ten-year target (for 1973-4) should be 390 000 places in total: 219 000 in universities, 122 000 in colleges of education and 51 000 in further education. (The 1962-3 figures were 216 000 in total, of which 118 000 were in universities, 55 000 in teacher-training and 43 000 in further education.) Higher education for adults should be encouraged – for retraining and refresher purposes as well as for those needing a second chance.

Staffing and students
Student-staff ratios in higher education should not be allowed to deteriorate (in 1961-2 there were the following ratios: 7.6:1, universities; 10:1 in English and 16:1 in Scottish teacher-training colleges; 7.1:1 on English and 9.1:1 on Scottish advanced further education courses).

Wastage rates should be a reflection of the students' abilities, and not at a certain fixed proportion. (At the time of the report it was about fourteen per cent in universities, seven per cent in teacher training and up to sixty per cent in sectors of further education.) Wastage in further education might be cut by the provision of a wider range of degree level courses and more attention to teaching methods.

There should be residential accommodation for two-thirds of the additional students coming into higher education.

Fees should be increased to meet twenty per cent of costs, instead of the 1962-3 level of eleven per cent in universities, six per cent in further education. Loans should not be introduced in the immediate future.

Government
At the level of the institution, more powers should be given to academics.

Nationally, the Grants Commission, which would be responsible for advising the government on the needs of all the autonomous institutions of higher education, should be a buffer institution, like the University Grants Committee between the universities and the government. The commission should not be accountable to Parliament.

The government should be advised on salaries by an independent body. The Committee of Vice-Chancellor and Principals should be strengthened.

There should be a Minister of Arts and Science responsible for the Grants Commission, the research councils and similarly constituted bodies. Responsibility for other higher education institutions should remain with the Minister of Education (in Scotland, the Secretary of State) and local education authorities.

Short-term emergency
To cope with the 'bulge' generation in 1966-7, the government should enable universities to provide for ten per cent more places than planned by stepping up capital and recurrent grants.

Universities should consider using evening classes and correspondence courses as supplementary measures.

The Council for National Academic Awards should be set up immediately.

The government should provide a national information service for higher education opportunities to work in conjunction with the Universities Central Council on Admissions and the clearing house for teacher-training colleges.

A standing consultative council should also be appointed straight away. This would enable continuous consultations between the three ministries concerned with higher education and the Grants Commission.

Action on the report

The statement from the Conservative government issued immediately after the report accepted a number of the main recommendations. The most important were the target figures for the whole of higher education and for universities in 1967-8 and 1973-4. It also agreed to meet the estimated cost. With these targets, the government accepted the assumption that higher education should be available to the able and willing. It also agreed that the colleges of advanced technology and two Scottish central institutions should become universities, and that the Royal College of Art and the College of Aeronautics should be financed through the UGC.

The government strongly supported the report's emphasis on scientific and technological studies and said that it would get an early report on the building up of three existing colleges as specialised science universities

(Imperial, London; Manchester and Strathclyde); and also on the proposal for a new technological university. It also accepted the proposal for a Council for National Academic Awards and agreed that a body on the lines of the UGC should continue as a buffer between government and individual universities. The government promised to review university finance later.

Shortly afterwards, the government rejected the Robbins proposal for a minister of art and science. Instead, it accepted the minority recommendation of Sir Harold Shearman that there should be a secretary of state for education, with separate ministers of state for schools and higher education, including universities.

The 1964 Labour government made an almost immediate statement on the Robbins report. But so far from continuing to support the report, it was the first shot in a sustained campaign to overturn most of the Robbins recommendations. That statement, mainly concerned with teacher-training, was followed by important speeches by the Secretary of State, Anthony Crosland, at Woolwich and Lancaster in which he defined and defended the 'binary' policy: the policy of keeping administratively separate the autonomous universities and public sector colleges. In 1966 a White Paper, *A Plan for Polytechnics*, created the polytechnic structure: thirty polytechnics were proposed, incorporating colleges of technology, commerce and art.

The Labour government also rejected the proposal that colleges of education should integrate with universities. It would have no more new universities (apart from the colleges of advanced technology and the Sussex and 'greenfields' group then being established). It did not want SISTERs. It did not want colleges of further education queueing up for promotion to university status. The thirty polytechnics were to be a permanent top to the public sector ladder. These were to do degree work, much of which would overlap with universities but would in general be more 'vocational' or 'relevant'. The government backed the idea of the Council for National Academic Awards, not so much as an interim stage for colleges on the way to becoming universities, but as a means of giving high academic status to public sector work. The Labour government created the Open University, thus pioneering open access and cheap higher education for adults. Also, against the Robbins view, it decided that universities should be made accountable to Parliament: since 1968 the books of the UGC and individual universities have been open to the Comptroller and Auditor General and the Public Accounts Committee.

The CNAA and the Open University turned out to be two of the success stories of higher education during the 1960s and 1970s. The CNAA pattern of validating college proposals for courses was later copied for technician and business education (see page 6), as an effective way of guaranteeing

19

standards while encouraging some institutional freedom. The Open University, which took its first graduates in 1973, pioneered new forms of distance teaching for adults, using correspondence, radio and television and occasional personal contact. Its credit-based structure influenced a number of course developments in other universities and polytechnics.

The 1970 Conservative government followed the general lines of the Labour policy in its major policy statement, the 1972 White Paper, *Education: a Framework for Expansion*. It was designed to boost the public sector at the expense of the universities. On the explicit grounds that it was only a minority that wished to pursue the study of a subject to a scholarly level, and the implicit grounds of expense, the government proposed to cut down on the planned rate of expansion; to limit the proportion of university places in higher education so that they represented no more than a half, rather than the sixty per cent that Robbins recommended; and also to provide an alternative to the three-year single honours degree taken by the majority of students.

The government planned to provide for an annual intake of 200 000 into higher education (i.e., equivalent to almost the total higher education population when the Robbins committee was sitting). This would represent twenty-two per cent of the age group. By 1981, it expected that there would be 750 000 students in higher education in Great Britain, with a student-to-staff ratio of 10:1. The proportions in university and non-university institutions should be about equal. There would be places for 306 000 full-time university students, of whom seventeen per cent, as opposed to nineteen per cent in 1972, would be postgraduate, and a further 15 000 part-timers. It planned to expand polytechnic and other further education college places from the 1971 total of 204 000 to 335 000 by 1981. The polytechnics ought to be providing 180 000 of the places. With the impending drop in the school population, and thus a drop in demand for teachers, teacher-training places were to be cut back severely. The government proposed that the number of initial training places should be cut to 60 000–70 000, compared with the 1971 total of 114 000. They would, however, expect to do more in-service training, although the government's estimate of 15 000 or so places would not make up for its cutback in initial places.

The government's greatest innovation was to approve the James committee proposals (see page 47) for a two-year Diploma in Higher Education, to fill the gap between part-time courses, three-year full-time courses and some of the specifically vocational two-year courses. The government intended that Dip. HEs should be acceptable as a terminal qualification, or, on the basis of credits, enable a student towards more advanced qualifications.

As for the future structure of higher education, government planning would be conditioned by three principles: the need to avoid the proliferation of new institutions, where colleges already existed; the need for each institution to be large enough to provide higher education courses of an acceptable standard and range; and the expectation that, wherever possible, courses should be provided within reasonable reach of the homes of part-time students.

Although it was prepared for colleges of education to merge with universities, the government did not expect that many would do so, because universities would have had to cut their own rate of expansion to keep within the total growth rate allowed by the government.

The Conservative government left outstanding the matter of a revised form of control of public sector for higher education. The 1974 Labour government set up a committee under a minister of state, Mr Gordon Oakes, whose report was expected in early 1978. The report was confidently predicted to recommend the establishment of a national grants committee with much the same functions as the University Grants Committee and parallel to it. This would negotiate a total grant from the government to meet eighty-five per cent of the costs of public sector higher education, and which would then be responsible for distributing grants to individual institutions.

The 1974 Labour government significantly reduced the higher education target figures. In 1974 it proposed that the Conservative target of 750 000 places for 1981 (twenty-two per cent of the age group) be reduced to 650 000. In the White Paper *Public Expenditure 1978-80* (HMSO, 1976) it further reduced the target to 600 000. This was expected to cater for about fifteen per cent of the age group. The reduction in teacher-training places would not account for more than half the decrease. The cutback therefore implied some increase in the competition for entry for some subjects: a break with the Robbins principle accepted until then, that places should be provided for all those with the appropriate qualifications who wanted to continue their studies.

During that period, universities in particular were the victims of a stop-go policy. They had suffered under the Conservative government decision in 1973 not to compensate them for inflation. The Labour government, while paying some supplement, reduced the agreed grants for the following years as part of its public expenditure cuts, and because there appeared to be less student demand. But with the expenditure White Paper for 1981-2 (HMSO, 1978), universities' expenditure was projected to rise faster than that for education as a whole.

In general then, higher education developed quite differently from the way the Robbins committee recommended. The scale was greater: though perhaps it was not surprising that back in 1963 the committee should have underestimated the effects of introducing universal secondary education, and especially comprehensive education. The structure was divided, against the Robbins view of the spectrum in which the further education colleges would move up to enlarge the university sector. Those merged in the 1970s when their numbers were reduced joined other colleges of education or polytechnics. The colleges of education were not federated with the universities. Universities themselves rejected the Robbins view that they should provide more general undergraduate degrees. Thus, the lessening of specialisation of the secondary school curriculum, another Robbins objective, was doomed to fail unless universities took up the Dip. HE.

By 1977, it was clear that there would be further major changes within higher education for reasons undreamt of when the Robbins committee was set up. The system might have to contract. By the mid-1980s, the smaller age-groups passing through the schools would have reached higher education, a trend which would follow on from a voluntary dropping-off in the number of applications to higher education in the later 1970s. Despite some speculation that comprehensive secondary education would continue to boost the proportion of the age group wanting higher education, it was noticeable that a number of institutions were beginning to take an interest in adults as a potential source of customers.

CHILDREN AND THEIR PRIMARY SCHOOLS

report of the Central Advisory Council (England)
vol I   report   1967 HMSO   £1.50
vol II   appendices 1967 HMSO   £1.87

Chairman: Lady Plowden
Members: Sir John Newsom, Mr H. G. Armstrong, Prof. A. J. Ayer,
Miss M. F. M. Bailey, Mrs M. Bannister, Miss M. Brearley, Dr I. C. R. Byatt,
Hon. Mrs J. Campbell, Prof. D. V. Donnison, Miss Z. E. Dix, Prof. C. E.
Gittins, Miss S. E. Gray, Mr E. W. Hawkins, Miss E. M. Parry, Mr A. Puckey,
Mr T. H. F. Raison, Ald. E. V. Smith, Mr R. T. Smith, Prof. J. M. Tanner,
Brig. L. L. Thwaites, Mr T. H. Tunn, Mr M. H. Wilson, Mr F. M. White,
Dr M. Young *plus* Mr P. Mursell and Mr H. B. Rose (who both resigned).
Department of Education and Science and HMIs: Miss S. M. Duncan, HMI;
Miss N. Goddard (seconded); Mr D. T. Jones, HMI; Mr J. E. H. Blackie, HMI;
Mr D. H. Leadbetter; Miss E. M. McDougall, HMI; Miss M. E. Nicholls, HMI,
(assessors); Mr M. Kogan (secretary).

Terms of reference: To consider primary education in all its aspects and
the transition to secondary education.

With all the impetus of the 1944 Education Act directed towards
establishing secondary education for all, primary education had been out
of the political limelight for twenty years or more. Plowden changed all
that with its revelation of how primary education had been developing and
its general support for the trends; and for its advocacy of two new ideas:
far more parental involvement in their children's education, and the
redistribution of some educational resources to compensate for social and
economic deprivation, in what it called 'educational priority areas.'
   The changing technology of school building which made the new schools
of the 1950s and 1960s such bright and open places was an apt symbol of
many of the changes going on inside the schools. Increasingly children
were being encouraged to find and test things for themselves, and develop
all their expressive skills. Dickensian rote learning seemed a long way away.
Plowden expressed cautious support. It wanted to extend the experience
of 'good normal primary schooling,' which it saw as including such
'genuine virtues' as 'neatness, accuracy and perseverance.' It was scarcely
the advocacy of anarchy which critics began to suggest within a year or
two of publication. But the criticisms have had a lasting effect (see the
Bullock report, page 58).
   Plowden had commissioned research on the attainment of children

related to such home and school characteristics as the degree of parental involvement in their children's education, the home environment and the state of the school. It had shown that parental attitudes exerted the greatest influence. Plowden therefore suggested ways to involve all parents, especially those who did not usually turn up to meetings with teachers, recognising that a change in teachers' attitudes might be required.

With its suggestion for positively discriminating in favour of 'educational priority areas,' Plowden made a lasting contribution to government anti-poverty policy. It developed the Newsom theme (see page 9) of the economic and social deprivations suffered by many of the children living in the poor and dying areas of town and country: the high rates of unemployment and delinquency, the low rates of educational attainment in general.

Plowden thought that about a tenth of the population was deprived in such ways. Notably among the Central Advisory Council reports, it produced a strategy. Although, as it noted, 'equality has an appealing ring, discrimination has not,' it argued strongly for giving special help to deprived areas, so that children there might be in a more realistic position to take advantage of the equality of opportunity that the education system was supposed to offer.

Plowden proposed the designation of 'educational priority areas' which should have the best that the system could offer. They should be the first on building lists, the first to have extra teachers and extra equipment allowances. They should be pioneers for some of the innovations. They could, for instance, be the first to benefit from the extension of nursery education. Although 'equality of opportunity, even when it means weighting the scale to reduce inequalities, still results in inequalities,' said Plowden, 'coupled with a commitment to the highest educational standards, it is the touchstone to apply.'

Plowden was also keen that teachers should get much more help. Secretaries, school meals assistants and playground helpers should take over some of the more obviously non-professional tasks of teachers. Some classroom duties should be delegated to aides: trained assistants under the teacher's control.

The report marked a high point of optimism as to how reforming education would bring about social change. The Plowden report showed school as a form of salvation: at any rate the schools which encouraged close links with homes, and the free, creative and child-centred approach which had made many infant schools such notable places. Corporal punishment should, of course, go. Above all schools would need to recognise that 'learning is a continuous process from birth.' This suggestion that learning outside school is as potent and valid as learning inside was remarkable in such a report.

24

Unlike most of the Central Advisory Council reports, Plowden was a politically sophisticated document. It worked out strategies, ordered priorities. As the council said, the recommendations called for additional money and labour at almost every point. Such costs were inevitable, in its view, if a service of the size and complexity of primary education was to reach maximum efficiency and effectiveness. Plowden set an example for its successors in recognising that choices had to be made. Its order for the following ten years: the establishment of educational priority areas, the introduction of teachers' aides, the improvement of bad primary school building, the extension of nursery education and then the changes in the ages and stages of primary education.

Main recommendations

Home, school and neighbourhood
Schools, local education authorities and the Department of Education should encourage all parents into a far more active involvement in their children's education.

There should be experiments with community schools – schools open beyond school hours for pupils and their parents – starting with priority areas. There should be positive discrimination in favour of such schools as a matter of national policy. About ten per cent of pupils should be covered at the end of five years, possibly more later. At designated schools no class should exceed thirty, teachers should get a £120 salary addition, aides should be enrolled, one to every two classes. EPAs should have priority on building programmes, they should get extra books and equipment and they should be the first to benefit from the expansion of nursery education.

There should be research to see which EPA developments had the most constructive effects, so as to assist in planning the longer-term programme. More efforts should be made to improve educational opportunities for the children of immigrants. Teacher training (initial and in-service) should make teachers aware of the cultural background and language problems of immigrants. Relevant curricular developments should be expanded. There should be more courses for immigrant teachers, and schools with special language problems or other difficulties associated with immigrants should be generously staffed: there might be more experiments using student volunteers.

There should be changes in the school health and welfare services. Medical examinations should be on a more selective basis. Observation registers should be set up. Schools should have social workers attached. Education welfare officers should be trained to carry out wider social work functions. Some of their minor duties should be carried out by a new grade of welfare assistant. There should be experimental schemes for the joint training of teachers and social workers.

HM Inspectorate should undertake ten-yearly surveys of primary education.

Structure of primary education

In view of the importance of the pre-school years, nursery education should be provided part-time for most, and full-time for about fifteen per cent of children in the three to five age-range. It should probably take in not more than half the three-year-olds but as many as ninety per cent of the four-year-olds. Responsibility for day nurseries should be transferred from the Ministry of Health to the Department of Education. There should be one qualified teacher to every sixty children: the main day-to-day work should be in the hands of two-year trained assistants, in the ratio of one to every ten children. Ideally, all services for the care of young children should be grouped near the children's homes and the primary school.

The ages and stages of primary education should be as follows: the normal school starting age should be the September term following the child's fifth birthday, and children should be allowed to attend half-time only, until the age of six. But this should only happen once nursery education had been expanded to provide one year for all who want it. (The new primary starting age would mean a later entry date for two-thirds of the children.) There should be some flexibility on ages of transfer but, in general, children should go on to the infants (to be renamed first) school at the age of eight. They should be there for three years and in the junior (to be renamed middle) school for four years. Consequently, transfer to secondary education should be at twelve plus.

Until the expansion of nursery education, and until the government was ready to announce national policy on the ages and stages, there should be interim changes in the starting date for primary schooling: February to August-born children should start school the September following their fifth birthday, the rest should start in the following April. Schools should be allowed to space their admissions over half a term and children should be allowed to attend half-time for up to two terms before full-time entry. The changes in the starting age would require legislation.

There should be more continuity between the stages of education. This could be achieved by more contact with parents, by organising teacher training to overlap more than one stage and by providing each child with a progress folder to accompany him through school.

Except in the case of small rural or small voluntary schools, first and middle schools should not normally be combined. The most satisfactory size for new first schools would be two-form entry (240 pupils) and for middle schools, two- or three-form entry (up to 400 pupils). In rural areas, schools with a five to eleven age-range should have at least three classes, each covering two age groups.

Curriculum and internal organisation
National attainment should be measured by recurring surveys (like the Department's reading survey and the National Foundation for Educational Research's reading and maths surveys). Secondary schools should inform primary schools of their pupils' progress.

The law on the act of worship should be interpreted more freely. Corporal punishment, defined as the infliction of physical pain, should be forbidden in maintained schools. It should be a condition of the registration of independent schools that they would not use it. The first would require a change in the school regulations, the second in the law. Until the change in the law, no independent school using corporal punishment should be eligible for recognition as efficient.

Primary school work should combine class and individual methods (the committee welcomed the development of child-centred methods). The maximum class size should be reduced from forty but there should be experimental grouping of several classes for certain activities. Non-streaming, established in the infants school, should spread through the junior age groups.

Handicapped children should be the subject of a detailed enquiry. Counselling services should be provided for their parents. The term 'slow learner' should be substituted for 'educationally subnormal.'

Long-term studies should be made of gifted children.

Staffing
There should be more efforts to encourage teachers, men especially, into primary education, and training should overlap the stages of the system. The employment of part-time teachers should be encouraged and satisfactory conditions of service negotiated for them. The employment of part-time teachers in well staffed areas could release full-time teachers for more difficult areas.

More effective use should be made of meals assistants, welfare assistants and secretaries.

Trained teachers' aides should be employed under the supervision of qualified teachers in the ratio of one full-time aide to 60–80 infants (two classes) and 120–160 juniors (four classes). A national scheme for their employment should be accompanied by an assurance that aides would not be used to dilute the qualified teaching force.

Head teachers should teach.

The HM and local education authority inspection system should continue.

There should be a full enquiry into teacher training: the influence of colleges of education and university departments is unusually great at a time of rapid expansion and rapid staff turnover.

Nursery assistants (working with children up to the age of five or six) and teachers' aides (for the five to thirteen age-range) should have a training based on the National Nursery Examination Board experience. Young students should take a two-year course, three-fifths of which would be spent on practical work. Entrants over twenty-one should be able to take a one-year course, four-fifths of which would be practical.

Independent schools

The government should consider requiring independent schools to state in their prospectuses whether they are recognised as efficient, or merely registered, and it should devise more informative terms. Criteria for registration should be raised. All head teachers should be qualified.

Buildings and equipment

The government should allow for an extra £7–10 million annually over a seven-year period, starting in 1971, in the minor works building programme, to enable primary schools to get rid of their worst deficiencies. Authorities saving money on individual major works should be allowed to spend it on minor works. Head teachers should have more freedom in spending.

Status and government of primary education

Differences between primary and secondary schools should be eliminated or narrowed: for instance, maximum class size, equipment and building place allowances.

Teachers should be represented on local education committees and sub-committees concerned with primary education.

School managers should be appointed for educational, not political, reasons. Parents of children attending the school should be represented. As far as possible, schools should have individual managing bodies; where grouped, the groups should be small. The appointment of head teachers should be considered one of their most important tasks and they should be prepared to take expert advice.

The opinions of head teachers should not be ignored on such issues as building programmes for their schools and out-of-hours use of their premises.

Action on the report

Although ten years after publication, Plowden recommendations were still being acted on, the report initially seemed to get off to a bad start. Before the council finished its work, the Labour government took a decision on part of the Plowden brief: the age of transfer. In 1966, pressed by local education authorities trying to make plans for secondary reorganisation, the Secretary of State, Anthony Crosland, said that he would willingly consider middle school schemes and transfer ages of eight or nine and twelve or thirteen, thus pre-empting a careful (but probably unrealistic) argument from Plowden.

It was also a time of public expenditure cuts. The best that Plowden got out of the 1964 Labour government was a £16 million special building programme, spread over two years, to replace schools in priority areas (in addition to an ordinary school building programme of £85 million); the reference to the Burnham committee to consider the question of salary additions for teachers in such schools; and the funding of a three year action research programme to define an EPA policy. Within a year of publication there was a Burnham agreement that teachers in 570 primary schools of 'exceptional difficulty' should have a salary addition (£120) and the DES and the Social Science Research Council had produced £175 000 for the research programme (see page 32).

The Conservative government (1970–74) vastly extended the chances of building in priority areas, without specifying this as an object. Mrs Margaret Thatcher got agreement for a £112 million programme to replace primary schools built before 1903. Starting in 1973–4 and spread over three years, this was the biggest-ever building improvement programme. It also fitted conveniently with the government's wish not to build comprehensive schools. One measure of the scale of the Thatcher task was that even by 1976 it was still reckoned that there were a million children in schools built before 1903.

The Conservative government took another historic step with the White Paper, *Education: a Framework for Expansion* (1972) when it reversed the policy which had prevented almost all development of nursery education after 1960, except on the small scale made possible since 1969 by the Urban Programme. The government followed the Plowden prescription, in aiming to provide for ninety per cent of four-year-olds and fifty per cent of three-year-olds. It launched a £30 million building programme, estimating that 400 000 new places would be needed in addition to the 300 000 already existing. There would also need to be an increase of 15 000 teachers bringing the total to 25 000. Although the White Paper welcomed diversity of provision – nursery classes, schools, playgroups, and day nurseries – it expected that most places would be provided in nursery classes attached to infant schools.

That made demographic sense. It was already clear that primary school numbers would be falling dramatically during the late 1970s, and that teachers and space would both be available. However, the White Paper only just preceded a series of public expenditure cuts by the outgoing Conservative government and incoming Labour government. Despite encouragement not to sacrifice the nursery programme, it was clear that local education authorities were not going to be enthusiastic about incurring loan sanction for new projects when they could not continue to support existing commitments.

The Conservative government also took up the Plowden recommendations to look at teacher education and training, and at the education of handi-capped children. On the first it appointed a small, almost full-time, committee under the chairmanship of Lord James (see page 45); on the second, it appointed a committee more like the Central Advisory Council, under the chairmanship of Mrs Mary Warnock, whose report was expected in 1978.

On returning to office in 1974, the Labour government reinstated positive discrimination as an objective of policy, for example in building programmes and the distribution of the rate support grant. It also set up one unit in the Department on the assessment of performance (see page 62) and another on educational disadvantage, which was planned to work closely with a government-funded centre for information and advice on educational disadvantage established at Manchester, with the brief of advising on curriculum and teaching methods relevant to those who were underachieving or were otherwise educationally disadvantaged. Both unit and centre were targets of constant criticism. The unit was only in the public eye for running a series of seminars. The centre appeared to lack any initiative. It was accused of telling people what they were already doing.

Combined with the pressure from the Bullock report, the government took up the proposals on monitoring (see page 60), and the HM Inspectorate began in 1975 a series of visits to over 500 schools to obtain a broad picture of the work of children aged seven, nine and eleven in maintained primary schools. The survey looked at language and literacy, mathematics, science, aesthetics and social development. It was being complemented by a National Foundation for Educational Research project on their reading, and a series of mathematics tests for the eleven-year-olds. The HMI survey was due to be published in 1978.

It also set up the Taylor report on school government (see page 63) which was its response to pressure which built up in the 1960s and early 1970s for increasing parental participation in the running of schools.

A number of school health matters of interest to Plowden got picked up by the Court committee (*Fit for the Future*, report of the committee on child health services appointed by the Secretary of State for Social Services, HMSO, 1977), though the terms of reference excluded one of the most controversial questions: whether the school health service should become once more a local education authority responsibility.

Mrs Shirley Williams, as Secretary of State, reaffirmed in the 1977 Green Paper, *Education in Schools, a consultative document*, the government's commitment to giving 'special help to children disadvantaged by social, environmental or other handicaps,' recognising that this 'might require positive discrimination in the use of resources.' She also took up other Plowden matters, reopening the question of corporal punishment by asking for views from teachers, parents and others interested, since only one authority (the Inner London Education Authority) had banned it in primary schools, and at least one-third of the 104 authorities did not lay down any restrictions at all on its use.

On the other hand, the Secretary of State tried to close the question of a compulsory act of worship, by saying that the law would not be changed.

The Secretary of State also took up the question of parents' rights, following ten or more years' campaigning by such pressure groups as the Advisory Centre for Education and the Confederation for the Advancement of State Education, and in line with the 1977 Green Paper statement, that 'parents should be given much more information about the schools, and should be consulted more widely.' It was a Labour government which had set up the Taylor committee on school governors, and in response to which Mrs Williams said she agreed with the recommendation that parents should be represented. She also issued a circular in 1977 to give local education authorities guidance on the facts that they should make available in writing to parents about individual schools in their area and the arrangements schools should make to ensure that parents can consult teachers and be kept informed of their children's progress.

The government continued to encourage local education authorities to develop their nursery provision, recognising that although the opportunities for new building would be very restricted, there would be many opportunities for them to use existing primary school buildings as the primary school population fell from 4.7 million in 1977 to an estimated 3.9 million in 1982. The government also promised a circular on better coordination between the Department of Health and Social Security and the Department of Education on provision for the under-fives.

By 1977 it was clear that the style of primary school teaching had not shifted anywhere near as far as Plowden would have liked or critics had suggested. Research by Neville Bennett (*Teaching Styles and Pupil Progress*,

Open Books, 1976) showed not just that primary schools effectively had a common curriculum, but just how few used it in a progressive way: when they did so in a thorough manner, the attainments of pupils were higher than in conventional schools. In 1977, in a preview of the HMI primary survey (see page 62), the senior chief inspector went further in saying that there was a not altogether healthy 'narrowing of the definition of the basic skills and a risk of their separation within the curriculum.'

It was also clear by the late 1970s that the essential elements of the educational priority area scheme had substantially influenced subsequent government policy. A series of inner-city and deprived area projects combined positive discrimination of resources with the interdisciplinary styles of working recommended by Plowden. But compensatory programmes went through a difficult period in the early 1970s. Unrealistic expectations that disadvantage could be overcome almost instantly, by interventionist measures, were dashed in the wake of American experience and the joint Department of Education-Social Science Research Council programme of action research (*Educational Priority, EPA Problems and Policies*, HMSO, 1972). Nevertheless, the four DES-SSRC teams, under the national direction of Dr A. H. Halsey, concluded that:

● an EPA, despite its difficulties of definition and the fact that there are more deprived children outside EPAs than in, was a socially and administratively viable unit;

● preschooling was the outstandingly economic and effective device in the general approach to raising educational standards. Halsey thought that there should be a locally determined pattern in which playgroups and various forms of day care should be linked with LEA nursery classes;

● community schooling was shown to have powerful implications for community regeneration. Curricular implications apart, it needed a reform of school government and management schemes to make community involvement a reality;

● there were practical ways of improving the partnership between homes and schools in EPAs: in part by making the school more conscious of its public image, in part by extending the educational visitor idea, and in part by encouraging parents into schools.

● there were practical ways of improving the quality of teaching in EPA schools. The report claimed that teachers' morale had improved in the project areas. The teams found that the children's attainments were disturbingly low but that the West Riding reading scheme had raised reading levels substantially. Beyond that, the report argued for curriculum being far more concerned than it had traditionally been with the 'critical and constructive adaptation of children to the actual environment in which they live.' EPA education 'is about moving on, not standing still';

- action research was an effective method of policy formation and practical innovation;
- an EPA strategy could be no more than a part of a comprehensive social movement towards community development.

It was suggested that an EPA strategy might also lead to an improvement of children's attitudes to teachers and to learning (ILEA 1977). But during the mid-1970s, the difficulties of defining disadvantaged schools and disadvantaged teachers, and of attributing any effect to the extra payment of up to £276 to teachers, led local authorities to oppose the principle of special payments and led even the teachers' unions to suggest that the money might be better spent on resources.

PUBLIC SCHOOLS COMMISSION

reports of the commissions appointed by the Secretary of State for Education and Science

First report: on the independent boarding schools
1968 HMSO £1.16½

Chairman: Sir John Newsom
Members: Dame Kitty Anderson, Lord Annan, Dr K. Bliss, Mr J. C. Dancy, Mr J. Davies, Prof. D. V. Donnison, Dr T. E. Faulkner, Dame Anne Godwin, Mr W. S. Hill, Mr T. E. B. Howarth, Dr H. G. Judge, Mr G. H. Metcalfe, Prof. J. Vaizey, Prof. B. Williams.
Secretary: G. F. Cockerill.

Terms of reference: To advise on the best way of integrating the public schools with the state system of education.

In carrying out its tasks the commission will be expected to pay special attention to the following objectives: to ensure that the public schools should make their maximum contribution to meeting national educational needs, and in the first instance any unsatisfied need for boarding education ... to create a socially mixed entry ... to move towards a wider range of academic attainment amongst public school pupils, so that the public school sector may increasingly conform with the national policy for the maintained sector, to co-operate closely with the local education authorities in seeking to match provision with need for boarding education; to ensure the progressive application of the principle that the public schools, like other parts of the educational system, should be open to boys and girls irrespective of the income of their parents.

There are less than 300 of the mis-named public schools. Boarding schools for the most part, charging fees which exclude all but the rich or the subsidised, they are members of either the Headmasters' Conference, or the Governing Bodies' Association or the Governing Bodies of Girls' Schools' Association. With around 60 000 pupils, they cater for less than 1.5 per cent of the total school population. For generations they have been denounced and praised with equal extravagance.

In the 1940s, the public schools themselves were so anxious not to be isolated from the developing state provision that they pressed for some form of integration. But neither government nor local education authorities could approve a solution on the public schools' terms: this was essentially the case with the 1944 Fleming report which wanted to provide all parents with a free choice, unfettered by financial constraints and unconcerned about the impact on local systems.

The year 1964 saw the pendulum swing the other way. The Labour party's return to power after thirteen years in opposition revived a long-standing urge to abolish the public schools completely. It could be seen as a quirk of history that when the governments of France and Prussia were building up their national systems of secondary education in the nineteenth century, Britain was leaving it to private enterprise to prepare young people for the pick of prestigious jobs. That was no reason for keeping the schools for ever.

The schools were socially divisive, Labour critics claimed with reason: a chart in the commission's report was to show that public school pupils, statistically almost too small a group to identify at the age of fourteen, made up the largest proportion of the country's judges, bishops, leading doctors, directors of big firms, heads of Oxford and Cambridge colleges, Conservative members of Parliament and heads of the armed services. The schools appeared to be increasing their hold over the top ranks of the civil service. The products of six schools above all dominated these influential jobs: Eton, Winchester, Harrow, Rugby, Marlborough and Charterhouse.

The schools were also financially privileged, benefitting from substantial tax concessions as charities, which have freed them from income tax, corporation tax and capital gains tax; they also have had a fifty per cent reduction in rates. Additionally they have gained from tax devices to reduce the full impact of fees.

Nevertheless, the Labour Secretary of State for Education and Science, Mr Anthony Crosland, was widely seen to be signing his political death warrant when he established a commission to examine the public schools. What hope could there be of a consensus report?

The commission's terms of reference show that the government trod with care. It was not open to the commission to recommend the abolition of the public schools. It was in practice impossible to recommend their integration. As the commission said, the cost would have been prohibitive and out of proportion to the urgent claims for finance put forward by other sectors of the education system. Nor was there any evidence that local education authorities needed anything like the number of boarding places available.

Comforting themselves with the thought that 'educational reform in this country is always an untidy patchwork,' the commission therefore aimed to reduce the schools' social divisiveness by encouraging, and possibly requiring, them to make at least half of their places available to pupils assisted from public funds, and those who could be identified as in need of boarding educations.

This was too strong for public school members of the commission, who signed a note of dissent arguing that the recommendations paid 'insufficient regard to the continuing interests of the fee payers ... not a negligible or undesirable section of the community.' They also thought that the proposals would turn a number of 'exceptionally good grammar schools and outstandingly good academic boarding schools' into 'much less effective institutions in terms of their academic facilities and potential.'

A fourth dissenter, Professor Vaizey, accepted the main conclusions but forthrightly exposed the dilemma the commission itself had tried to ignore. The commission was allowing itself to be diverted from the central question: what should be the future of independent educational institutions drawing their pupils from a restricted social group? It was also landing itself with insuperable practical difficulties. 'The main objection to the private schools is that they are socially divisive. Some of them happen to have beds. It therefore seems less revolutionary to change the bodies in the beds than eliminate the beds.' It was, he suggested, as if Henry VIII had decided not to dismantle the monasteries but to fill them with social need cases who wanted a contemplative life. There was no evidence of a large unrecognised area of boarding need. He feared the commission's scheme would turn out to be a way of putting pressure on local authorities to help private schools prop up enfeebled finances, distracting the authorities from their main duty of taking decisions about the educational future of pupils, in the context of an established set of priorities in educational expenditure.

Main recommendations

Integration
Independent boarding schools suitable and willing to enter an integrated sector should be given every encouragement to do so. There should be a first condition that a school should be prepared to make up to half its places available to assisted pupils from maintained schools by the end of a seven year period.

Most schools, especially boys' schools, should admit pupils of a wider range of ability. Where schools are too small to admit pupils of widely differing ability they should adapt to the comprehensive system by shortening their courses and adjusting their ages of admission.

There might be a few exceptions: a very small number might cater wholly or mainly for sixth form pupils, one or two might cater for children with special aptitudes in music or ballet. Proposals to cater entirely for gifted children should be viewed with considerable caution but should not be excluded.

Some of the large boys' schools should be encouraged to go co-educational to meet the wishes and convenience of parents, and to provide more boarding opportunities for girls.

Independent boarding schools should be encouraged to work closely, not only with each other, but with maintained day schools with which they might share teaching resources and other facilities. For schools wishing to come within the maintained system there should be opportunities for aided status (a relationship with the state equivalent to voluntary aided schools), possibly in association with a central body rather than a local education authority. There should be an exchange of teachers between the maintained and independent boys' schools to match that already taking place in girls' schools.

Denominational schools
Although Christian foundations should be encouraged to accept pupils from other denominations, there should be safeguards for parents in matters of religious instruction and worship.

Changes at integrating schools
While important traditions and values should not be sacrificed, such as the importance of hard work, good pupil-teacher relationships and a wide variety of extra-curricular activity, there should be radical changes in styles: more women on the staff of boys' schools, more opportunities for pupils to pursue their personal interests, more alternatives to cadet force activities and games, more contact with home, more freedom of dress, no beating of boys by boys, no personal fagging.

Subsidies for private education
A majority recommended that action should be taken to end the fiscal and other charitable reliefs of schools which do not serve a truly charitable purpose.

Boarding need
The only justification for public expenditure on boarding education should be need for boarding, for either social or academic reasons. Social grounds would include circumstances in which a child is deprived of educational opportunities because of the absence of a home in this country or because of adverse family conditions.

By 1980, 45 000 assisted places should be provided in independent schools in England and Wales, 2000 in Scotland. (This was based on an estimate of 80 000 places needed: 20 000 places were already being paid for in whole or part from public funds.) All assisted pupils should attend schools approved for integration. As an interim measure, the commission would approve a scheme for 32 000 places, provided that this meant a smaller number of schools would be fully integrated, rather than a larger number of schools being only partially integrated.

Selection of assisted pupils
Guidance on boarding and placing policy should be given by the Boarding Schools Corporation to regional consortia of local education authorities which would handle the main volume of applications. The corporation would deal centrally with applications for sixth form colleges and from parents working overseas. Places should be offered in schools as near as possible to pupils' homes.

Assistance to parents
All assisted pupils, whatever their parents' means, should be entitled to free tuition equivalent to the average cost of education in maintained day schools. Parental contributions should be made according to means towards the remaining cost of an assisted place.

Finance
The cost of integrating 47 000 places was estimated to be £18.4 million annually, and of 32 000 places, £12.5 million annually.

Assistance from public funds for pupils (other than handicapped pupils) attending public schools should, after a date to be decided, be restricted to those attending schools accepted for integration.

Legislation and administration
An Education Act would be needed to enable an integrated sector to develop, under the guidance of a Boarding Schools Corporation. Schools should be invited to submit development plans as a basis for negotiation, but such schools would not automatically be accepted for integration. The Secretary of State should have the power in the last resort to compel a school to enter a scheme of negotiation. There should be provision for appeal.

Unrecognised schools
The commission endorsed the Secretary of State's decision to require all schools with boarding pupils to reach an efficient standard.

Action on the report

The history of this report amply exposed the insurmountability of a
Labour government's problems with the public schools. Abolition of the
whole independent sector has been out of the question; abolition of the
best and most prestigious part of it suicidal. But integration has also been
impossible in effect since the public schools are not dealing in any
commodity which the state would like, other than prestige. Professor
Vaizey's prognostications proved right. Nothing more was heard of the
Boarding Schools Corporation in either the period up to the 1970 election
when Labour lost office, or after 1974 when it returned.

The Labour government tried to tackle the more tangential question of
the financial privileges. In 1970 it introduced measures to abolish tax relief
on minors' income and on certain forms of insurance used to pay school
fees. (These measures were reversed by the Conservative government of
1970-74 and surprisingly were not reintroduced by Labour.) It would
have liked to prevent the use of life insurance policies for fee-paying but
was not able to work out a practical way to do this. In its 1974 manifesto
it said that it would deprive the schools of their charitable status.
Although delphic support came from an all-party House of Commons
Select committee in 1975 which suggested that educational 'charities'
should be able to prove that they are 'beneficial to the community,' again
there were grave practical difficulties.

The other more recent action by the government, chiefly aimed at
direct grant schools, was to announce that it would tighten up the
conditions on which a local education authority might send pupils,
other than handicapped pupils, to fee-paying schools. Following the
Education Act, 1976, which was designed to speed up progress to
comprehensive reorganisation, it issued a circular in July 1977. This said
that from September 1978, authorities would be authorised to take up
places in non-maintained schools only if they could show that there was
an absolute shortage of places or that pupils were assessed on grounds
unrelated to their ability and aptitude as needing boarding education.

Although independent schools as a whole were badly hit by the inflation
of the 1970s and the Houghton award on teachers' pay, and several closed,
the public boarding schools have continued to flourish. Enough parents
were clearly extremely happy to pay fees which, in 1977, were said to
average £1 750 a year.

M.T.D.A.E.—D

Second report: on independent day schools and direct grant grammar schools
1970 HMSO   90p

Chairman: Professor D. Donnison
Members: Mr C. R. Allison, Lord Annan, Miss K. Bliss, Mr T. E. Faulkner, Mr M. Arnold-Forster, Dame Anne Godwin, Mr W. S. Hill, Ald. F. H. Hutty, Dr H. G. Judge, Mr R. M. Marsh, Mr B. H. McGowan, Rev. Mother A. M. Reidy, Cllr. T. Taylor, Mr L. E. Waddilove, Miss J. Wilks, Prof. B. Williams, Very Rev. R. Woods, Mr R. W. Young.
Assessors: D. Evan Morgan, G. S. V. Petter.
Secretaries: D. Neylan, G. Etheridge.

Terms of reference: As for the first report and additionally: to advise on the most effective method or methods by which direct grant grammar schools in England and Wales and the grant aided schools in Scotland can participate in the movement towards comprehensive reorganisation and to review the principle of central government grant to these schools.

The commission was reconstituted and enlarged (and a parallel Scottish committee set up) to deal with the 178 direct grant schools and the 250 public day schools. It was a more realistic reference than that on the public boarding schools: but scarcely less controversial.

Up till the 1950s or 1960s, both sides of the political fence saw the direct grant schools as combining academic effectiveness with social virtue. Grammar schools, essentially, they provided free places for some clever children from poor families, and thereby enriched those children's chances.

Direct grant status has consisted of a government capitation grant (it was £84 for sixth formers, £32 for the rest in 1970 when the committee reported) provided that the school made at least twenty-five per cent of its places available without charge to those children educated for two years or more in a maintained primary school. Over and above such 'free places', local education authorities could take up 'reserved' places for which there was also no charge to parents, up to a total of fifty per cent of the school's places, and more, if the schools governors' agreed. Pupils taking up the residuary places, paid fees on a means-tested basis.

The public day schools have provided a similar sort of education on a fee paying basis: it was logical to examine the two types of school together.

The Conservative party went on believing in virtue: it later announced that it would like to extend the direct grant list (see page 44). But most of the Labour party turned hostile during the 1960s for two reasons. Direct grant schools did not appear to be providing much of a bridge between public and private sectors to benefit poor children; if anything the traffic was heavier the other way, enabling middle class children to have private education at the public's cost. Then, once the comprehensive policy was launched, the direct grant question became urgent: how could the government simultaneously promote one policy and subsidise its rival? And what, if anything, should it do about the independent day schools, similarly challenging their local schools?

The evidence of the Donnison commission came down on Labour's side. It found that three out of four of direct grant pupils came from white collar homes, three out of five from professional homes, only one in thirteen from a semi-skilled or a skilled worker's family, and also that there was a great range in the academic achievement of the schools. Only about a quarter of the direct grant schools lived up to the image of the grand academic school drawing the cleverest children from a large surrounding region. Many were Roman Catholic schools with a wide range of ability, and many were academically no different from the local authority maintained grammar school. So while direct grants might be less socially exclusive than the wholly independent schools, they were certainly more socially exclusive than the wholly maintained schools.

But the more urgent matter for educational policy was whether comprehensive reorganisation was better served by isolating these schools or by trying to integrate them. The commission was in no doubt. 'An educational system which enables a minority of the most fortunate children to take their education a long way while turning the rest out into the labour market as soon as it is socially tolerable for them to start work is as obsolete as the early industrial era from which it originated.' In comparing English and foreign secondary systems of education, it was struck that Britain was down at the bottom of the league table for sixth form provision, level with the equally selective Germany and the under-developed Italy. Belgium, France, Sweden and the Netherlands were a long way ahead. It foresaw a great upsurge in the demand for sixth form education as comprehensive education got into its stride. The help of 'good schools of every kind' would be needed. However, 'as reorganisation proceeds it becomes harder to make constructive use of the important contribution the direct grant schools could offer. Time is on no one's side.'

The commission went on to provide a detailed description of comprehensive education. But it came to few agreed conclusions on the direct grants' future, arguing that there could not be any blueprint, given the variety of local conditions and the differences in the direct grant schools themselves. It also failed to agree on the administrative and financial structure for integrating the direct grant schools. This was a disaster: mutual suspicions and jealousies had bedevilled relationships between

41

many direct grant schools and their local education authorities, ever since 1965 when Mr Anthony Crosland, the Secretary of State, had suggested they should discuss the possibilities of co-operation. It is an irony that a report which provided persuasive advocacy for a more rational approach to secondary reorganisation failed to provide a minister with the plan to finish the job.

Main recommendations

Participation in a comprehensive system

Day schools receiving grants from central or local authorities should participate in the move towards comprehensive reorganisation, in ways that accord with local needs and plans, by becoming: an eleven to eighteen comprehensive school, a component in a tiered system; a 'mushroom' school taking pupils at the lower secondary stage on a non-selective basis and taking in more pupils at sixth form level; a junior or sixth form college; a school providing for special needs (music etc.). Such arrangements should be worked out between schools and the local education authorities.

Direct grant schools unwilling or unable to participate in comprehensive reorganisation should be able to go independent.

Finance and status

The present direct grant arrangements should be ended. Day schools taking part in the comprehensive system should no longer charge fees.

Children already enrolled at the time of a school's change in status should be able to continue their education undisturbed.

Seven of the members (the direct grant interests) proposed that a Schools Grants Committee (taking over the functions of the Boarding Schools Corporation proposed in the first report) should make 100 per cent grants to participating schools, on the basis that staffing ratios, equipment and other resources should be no better and no worse than the general level for maintained schools with similar functions.

Eight of the members proposed that direct grant schools should adopt one of the forms of locally maintained status already available. The approved debts should be met from public funds.

Four members found both proposals acceptable in principle and thought that the choice should be made by the government in the light of reactions to the report.

Independent day schools

Independent day schools should be encouraged to participate in a comprehensive system on terms similar to those proposed for direct grant schools except that their capital debts should not normally be met from public funds.

The Secretary of State should issue guidance to local education authorities on their powers and duties to assist with, or pay, the fees of pupils at independent schools, so that arrangements should be more nearly uniform.

Gifted children

A majority of the commission recommended that academically gifted children should be educated within comprehensive schools. Five wished to preserve and develop a small number of highly selective schools on an experimental basis taking pupils from within the top two per cent of the ability range drawn from maintained or independent sectors.

Action on the report

There was no time for a Labour government to do anything about the recommendations before it lost the 1970 election. The Conservative government did not provocatively reopen the list: but nor did it take any notice of the report.

Eventually, with the 1974 Labour government, there was action on the report's simple and unanimous recommendation that direct grant status should be ended. But that government chose to go for isolation of direct grant schools, rather than their integration.

That kind of wooing changed no minds. By December 1976 only fifty-one direct grant schools had announced that they would like to join the maintained system. All but three of them were Roman Catholic schools, which had been expected to join, knowing that heavy debts would be paid off. The rest went to strengthen the independent sector, saving the state perhaps £15 million in capitation fees but depriving it of sixth form expertise.

It was a curious policy for a Labour government to pursue, though it was argued at the time that it was too late to work for integration. It was also suggested that many direct grant schools would not survive on independent status, especially those which had had more than fifty per cent of their places paid for by local education authorities under the old arrangements, and which would additionally be hit by the clauses of the Education Act, 1976, which made it much more difficult for local education authorities to send pupils to independent schools (see page 39). In 1976 local education authorities were assisting 1400 pupils at 104 of the ex-direct grant schools. The schools themselves gambled that they would easily attract parents willing to pay £600 or so a year, and a sufficient endowment income. Conservative education spokesmen in 1977 were suggesting that a Conservative government would restore direct grant status and really would reopen the list. In contrast, Conservative local education authorities made it clear that they did not want that political football kicked around again. But it was possible that the direct grant saga had still not ended in 1977.

TEACHER EDUCATION AND TRAINING

report of a committee appointed by the Secretary of State for Education
1972 HMSO 85p

Chairman: Lord James of Rusholme
Members: Miss E. Aggett, Mr C. English, Dr H. Judge, Mr P. Milroy, Mr J. F. Porter, Prof. J. R. Webster.
Assessor: Mr A. G. J. Luffman, HMI.
Secretary: Mr R. Dellar.

Terms of reference: In the light of the review currently being undertaken by the Area Training Organisations, and of the evidence published by the Select Committee on Education and Science, to enquire into the present arrangements for the education, training and probation of teachers in England and Wales, and in particular to examine: (i) what should be the content and organisation of courses to be provided; (ii) whether a proportion of intending teachers should be educated with students who have not chosen their careers or chosen other careers, (iii) what, in the context of (i) and (ii) above, should be the role of the maintained and voluntary colleges of education, the polytechnics and other further education institutions maintained by the local education authorities, and the universities, and to make recommendations.

James was a very different sort of enquiry from Plowden. The Plowden probing had left ministers, the DES and HMIs convinced that they deserved a respite before the next round. But there was an urgent need for some kind of enquiry. Colleges of education had expanded very quickly during the 1960s – 40 000 students in 1961, 120 000 ten years later – and some of the consequences needed investigating. The extension of the basic teacher-training course to three years had raised new expectations and caused new strains: there was a general demand for improved courses and improved staffing, and a degree of disillusion, as higher education became more competitive, with the isolated and inferior position of teacher training, subservient to university-dominated area training organisations. A fact much used by critics, who were beginning to complain also about children's lack of skill in reading (see page 58) was that students could be accepted into teacher training without even a GCE O level pass in English or mathematics.

But Mr Edward Short, the Labour Secretary of State, would only approve an enquiry in which the area training organisations were both prosecution and judge. In 1970 he asked them to make a report. Then Parliament set up a Select Committee enquiry as some sort of counter move in 1970–71. But it was as much a change of government, and the chance for Mrs Margaret Thatcher to fulfil a manifesto promise, that got the James enquiry established. Rather than reconvene the Central Advisory Council, Mrs Thatcher backed a new idea for education, the small and almost full-time committee.

The James committee did not collect new evidence for its report, since that was available, if somewhat inaccessibly, in the reports of the area training organisations and the Select Committee. James concentrated on producing a strategy starting from two assumptions: that teacher training should be closely linked with the needs of the schools, and that it should be an integral part of higher education. It was convinced that university domination had had a harmful effect on teacher training.

In arguing this way, James also introduced some new thinking to higher education. It wanted lifelong education, the possibility of a credit system and a commitment to a large degree of curricular freedom for colleges. In its thinking about the education of teachers, it gave authoritative backing to the view that all teachers should have a professional training of the same length and with a common general structure, whatever the type of school or age group for which they were trained. James thought that teachers in their first year of teaching should still be regarded as in training, and that more specialised matters, like the teaching of immigrants, should be left until they had had some school experience. The committee also backed the idea of an all-graduate profession. It wanted the work of colleges of education diversified so that they were no longer mono-technic and it made proposals for the control and co-ordination of teacher training and supply which would radically alter the existing structure, removing university institutes of education from their dominating position.

Main recommendations

Education and training
Professional training of all teachers should be the same in length and structure, however different in its emphasis and the details of its content. It should be organised in three cycles, the third of which, in-service training, should be given the highest development priority. The other two cycles, pre-service higher education and professional training, should extend over at least four years (i.e., to include the first, and so-called probationary, year of teaching).

These cycles should be regarded as consecutive parts of a continuous process. The objectives of pre-service education could then be sensibly determined, the professional training element kept closely in touch with the needs of the schools, and not made unnecessarily specialised, in the expectation that teachers would be able to have a further enriching training after some first-hand experience of teaching.

The first cycle should consist of a course of study leading to a higher education award recognised as a qualification for entry to the second cycle (e.g. a university or CNAA degree). Other specialist qualifications would be acceptable. There should be a two-year course leading to a new award, the Diploma in Higher Education. Although designed with the needs of teachers in mind, the DipHE should be widely acceptable to prospective students and employers alike.

The first year of the second cycle would normally be in a professional institution: a college of education or the education department of a university or polytechnic. The training would be specifically related to the teacher's needs in a first appointment. Successful students would be recommended to the Secretary of State for recognition as 'licensed teachers.' The second year of the cycle would consist of largely school-based training. Licensed teachers would be released for the equivalent of not less than one day a week for attendance at a professional institution or 'professional centre.' They would be able to look for advice to a teacher on the staff of their school, a 'professional tutor', who would also have particular responsibilities for co-ordinating the in-service training arrangements for all teachers in the school. Teachers successfully completing this year would become 'registered teachers', i.e. full members of the profession. All students successfully completing two years of professional training in the second cycle should receive the award of a professional degree of BA (Education).

During the third cycle, teachers should be entitled to release with pay, for in-service education and training on a scale not less than the equivalent of one term in every seven years, and, as soon as possible, on a scale of one term in five years.

Teachers for further education
The proposals on the licensing and registration of teachers would apply to teachers trained in the colleges of education (technical) who then proceeded to teach in schools, and should be applied to further education teachers if the further education system was aligned with schools. Third cycle opportunities should be available to further education teachers.

Administration, finance and the validation of awards
There should be strong regional agencies to administer the education and training of teachers, to expand third cycle work and organise a network of

professional centres. This pattern of regional bodies, Regional Councils for Colleges and Departments of Education, would modify the existing area training organisation system, but with considerably enlarged responsibilities. The new councils should represent all local institutions of higher education, and all those with an interest in teacher education and training. The administration of the regional councils should be financed by direct grant, in recognition of the fact that the councils' functions would extend beyond the university ambit, and that the financing of teacher education was largely drawn from non-university sources.

There should be a National Council for Teacher Education and Training to co-ordinate policy. All professional teaching qualifications, including the BA (Education), and all in-service professional awards, should be dependent upon recognition and approval by the national council. It should make recommendations to the Secretary of State on the recognition of 'licensed' and 'registered' teachers. It would also be empowered to award the BA (Education). Its professional committee would be the final arbiter on such questions as acceptable first cycle qualifications for admission to teacher training, and the Secretary of State should advise on professional qualifications.

National council decisions about the numbers of teachers needed by the schools would be incorporated in guidelines issued by the national council to regional councils, which would provide the framework for local policy.

The academic committee of the regional councils would be concerned with the first cycle work in the colleges with courses for the DipHE and the degree courses based upon the DipHE. The first awards of the DipHE should be made in 1975 and of the BA (Ed.) in 1977. The academic/ awarding function of the national council and the regional councils might be remitted to the Council for National Academic Awards or in some cases to universities.

The next steps
There should be a consultative document on the constitution, powers and geographical boundaries of the proposed regional councils.

The first students for the DipHE should be enrolled in September 1973. All intending teachers should embark on the new kind of second cycle courses in 1975 and the first awards of the BA (Ed.) should be made in 1977.

Local education authorities should begin to nominate professional tutors for their schools and further education colleges, to plan an expansion of third cycle activity, to study locations for possible professional centres and to take steps to develop suitable existing teachers' centres and professional centres. Local education authorities should appoint additional teachers,

48

and should be particularly generous to schools with a high turnover of staff.

Professional institutions should begin to redesign their courses.

Action on the report

The immediate reaction to James was that it proposed the destruction of the teacher training system. Its proposals for separating students' personal education from their professional training meant that the colleges of education would become indistinguishable from further education institutions. Mrs Thatcher's concern for a quick report scattered more fireworks around the educational world than any other considered here, except Robbins. But Robbins had the supreme good luck to report before an election, and at a time of expansion. The history of the James report was overshadowed by the need to cut back the teacher-training system to a degree that was unimaginable when the committee reported. It was an irony that five years after the report's publication, the teacher training system was beginning to look much as James would have wished.

The Conservative government in the White Paper, *Education: A Framework for Expansion* accepted the major James objectives if not the actual detail: the large expansion of in-service training, reinforcement of the teacher's probationary year, the progressive achievement of an all-graduate profession, improved training for teachers in further education, the integration of colleges of education into the higher education system, and improved arrangements for the control and co-ordination of teacher training and supply.

The government accepted in principle the committee's recommendation that teachers should be allowed a term off every seven years for retraining, beginning in 1974–5, and building up to three per cent of teachers being released at any one time by 1981. The government also agreed to support the DipHE by making it mandatory on local education authorities to make awards to DipHE students.

The government was not prepared to accept the full scale of the new probationary arrangements that James proposed, with the half way stage of 'licensed teacher' status, and the BA (Ed.) to be awarded at the end of it. It supported instead an eventual modification of the probationary year, and the use of professional tutors. This should begin on an experimental basis with the aim of producing a national scheme by 1975–6. Two areas were eventually designated. The government was opposed to a pattern of study and qualification which it thought would divorce teacher training from higher education. Thus it rejected the four-year BA (Ed.), but welcomed the introduction of a three-year ordinary degree, the B. Ed., incorporating educational studies, and designed to lead to qualified status. It thought some students might go on to a fourth year to a B. Ed. honours degree.

The government also rejected the proposals for regional and national machinery which, under the James scheme, would have wrested a number of powers from both government and universities, a matter taken up by the 1974 Labour government when it appointed a committee under Mr Gordon Oakes (see page 21). The Conservative government proposed to hold on to the control of supply. Until something better was produced, it would also hold on to the powers of professional recognition. It thought that academic validation should remain the responsibility of established academic bodies: the universities and the Council for National Academic Awards and the colleges themselves. That left the function of co-ordination, on which James succeeded, at least, in destroying the area training organisations. The government agreed that some modification was needed to ensure more representative regional machinery. It also, later, set up a new co-ordinating body: the Advisory Committee on the Supply and Training of Teachers.

But almost from that date, the future of teacher education and training was overshadowed by uncertainties, initially the failure of demand to match supply, then the 1973 public expenditure cuts, and most recently a continuing fall in the birthrate, bringing with it the knowledge that the school population was likely to go into almost permanent decline after 1977. The Conservative government issued a circular in 1973, based on unpublished information for the White Paper, suggesting that there should be a reduction in the number of full-time students in initial training from the 1973 level of 114 000 to 65 000 by 1981, and that a further 15 000 places should be allowed for in-service training.

The 1974 Labour government trimmed the figures even more. In a statement in March 1975 it was announced that, even taking into account policies designed to eliminate classes over thirty in the early 1980s, the continuing expansion of education for the under-fives and the programmes of induction and in-service training recommended by James, the non-university teacher-training places would have to be reduced to 60 000. This would mean the closure of thirty colleges.

But that was as nothing to the 1976 statement by Mrs Shirley Williams, as Secretary of State, that the total number of places would have to be reduced to 45 000, and that would include 10 000 places for in-service training. The intake of students would be slashed from the 1976 level of almost 30 000 to 12 000 in 1977, 10 000 in 1978. These cuts represented a sixty per cent contraction in the scale of teacher training, intended to match a projected fall in the school population during the 1980s of possibly 1.5 million, and the lower wastage rate among teachers. This, it was later announced, would mean the closure of twenty-eight colleges and the merger of fourteen more, so that teacher training would henceforward take place in seventy-five colleges (many of them merged with polytechnics) as opposed to the 162 colleges of education which existed in 1973.

It was argued by most critics that inevitably the merging of colleges with polytechnics, and the existence of the DipHE would mean that far more of those intending to become teachers would not have any professional training until after they had completed their personal education. It was only with the expansion of modular courses, aimed at a wider group of students than those wishing to teach, that the government could achieve a more efficient use of resources, and the opportunity to expand or contract the output of teachers as required.

The Green Paper of 1977, *Education in Schools, a consultative document* took a more optimistic line in suggesting that there was scope for raising standards of entry and for introducing other improvements. Although lack of resources precluded the development of four-year B. Ed. courses for all, the government thought that there should be graduate entry as a norm from 1979 or 1980, and that the normal minimum entry qualification to courses should be GCE A level passes in two subjects including qualifications in English and mathematics.

The government also revived the James idea of probationary status in saying that it expected to see the general spread of induction schemes with lighter time-tables for new teachers, within the following few years, with designated members of staff given special responsibility for overseeing the work of new teachers. There would be further discussions about the award of status and the contractual arrangements for new teachers.

Finally, it was confirmed that, even with the general cuts in resources, the government was still planning to expand in-service training: 'With the declining inflow of newly qualified teachers to schools... there is both opportunity and greater need for in-service training.' On 1977 figures it was expected that the numbers of teachers released for both in-service training and induction training would rise from the full-time equivalent of 4500 in 1977 to the full-time equivalent of 18 500 in 1981. There was little evidence in 1977, however, that local education authorities had done much to extend induction or in-service schemes.

ADULT EDUCATION: A PLAN FOR DEVELOPMENT

report of the committee appointed by the Secretary of State for Education and Science
1973 HMSO £1.90

Chairman: Sir Lionel Russell
Members: Mr C. H. Barclay, Mr J. Conway, Mr R. D. Salter Davies,
Mr T. Ellis, Mr B. Groombridge, Mr D. Heap, Mr J. W. Henry, Mr H. D.
Hughes, Prof. H. A. Jones, Mr H. J. Marsh, Ald. Mrs E. Mitchell, Dr E.
Monkhouse, Sir A. Owen.
Assessors: Mr F. A. Harper; Mr S. P. Whitley; Mr J. A. Lefroy, HMI;
Mr J. A. Simpson, HMI; Mr C. W. Rowland; Mr R. W. Evans, HMI.
Secretary: Mr E. E. H. Jenkins.

Terms of reference: To assess the need for and to review the provision of
non-vocational adult education in England and Wales; to consider the
appropriateness of existing educational, administrative and financial
policies; and to make recommendations with a view to obtaining the most
effective and economical deployment of available resources to enable adult
education to make its proper contribution to the national system of
education conceived as a process continuing through life.

About half the population leave school at the earliest opportunity. Very
few go back to formal education. Education for adults other than the
training and vocational courses for professional and other qualifications –
the so-called liberal adult education – retains a minority appeal. It also
remains the poor relation attracting little more than one penny in every
pound spent on education.

Characterised on publication as a mountain which had laboured long
and brought forth an overweight mouse, the Russell report was not able to
escape the slur of being altogether too modest. It also lacked the evidence
which had been such a feature of other educational reports and which had
enabled others to campaign on issues on which the committee itself had
been ambivalent.

Russell, it is true, wanted adult education to be widened in scope. 'Our
vision is of a comprehensive and flexible service of adult education, broad
enough to meet the whole range of educational needs of the adult in our
society. It must therefore be integrated with all the other sectors of the
educational system but at the same time firmly rooted in the active life of
local communities; and it must be readily accessible to all who need it,
whatever their means or circumstances.'

Russell saw adult education as having to meet three sorts of needs. People ought to have opportunities to continue with formal education, be it a second chance at GCE, or remedial help with reading, or an updating of their particular skills; they ought to have a chance to pursue creative studies; and they ought to be enabled to play a more active part in some of the many roles in which they find themselves as adults, ranging from consumer to trade unionist, school governor, voluntary worker or magistrate. Given that most adult education was of the second kind, the pursuit of 'liberal studies', Russell offered a more challenging perspective.

If translated literally, Russell might have had an impact on the educational experience of three-quarters of the adult population. For Russell maintained that its proposals were not a recipe for more of the same, but would effectively redress the existing provision to 'meet the individual and social needs of the educationally underprivileged who left school at or near the minimum leaving age.'

Russell however sidestepped the idea of a universal right to adult education implicit in the idea of permanent education, or recurrent education, which were by that time attracting both theoretical and practical interest in Europe and the USA. It was in favour of a study of paid educational leave, but, 'permanent education is a long term concept and we do not have time to wait for it.' Yet, the James committee, reporting earlier, had already proposed a form of recurrent education when it recommended one term off every seven years so that teachers could take the sort of course they wanted.

Russell was also extremely modest in its proposals for administrative change. It thought that the existing structure of local education authorities, the Workers Educational Association and the university extra-mural departments would be able to meet any new demands, with some better co-ordination, and a mere doubling of expenditure which would still mean that adult education took up less than one per cent of the national education budget. It was clear that much would turn on the influence of a national development council and local co-ordinating bodies to provide a stimulus for local innovation.

Main recommendations

Structure of adult education
Adult education should continue to be a partnership between statutory and voluntary bodies. The local education authority should be the main provider and should take the initiative in co-operative planning.

The government should take a lead by revising sections 41 and 42 of the Education Act, thus putting a positive duty on local education authorities to provide varied and comprehensive adult education. The Secretary of State should ask local education authorities to submit a development plan drawn up in consultation with other providing bodies; establish a widely representative development council for adult education in England and Wales; and should strengthen the administrative base within the Department of Education and Science and among HM Inspectors.

There should be regional advisory councils for adult education to encourage co-operation between local authorities and these should probably be sub-committees of the existing regional advisory councils for further education.

Locally there should be development councils to advise the local education authority. These should be widely representative of providers and users of education.

Local education authorities should provide grants and facilities for voluntary adult education activities in their area. They should expand opportunities for formal general education, recognising that they were major providers of courses. They should make special provision possibly for those who have traditionally taken little part in adult education.

Publicity should be much improved. Adult education should be served by area organisations easily identifiable by the public. Eventually the Secretary of State should introduce legislation on the running of such area organisations.

The direct grant principle should be maintained. Direct grants should be paid to major providing bodies like the universities and the Workers' Educational Association, to the long-term residential colleges and to such bodies as the National Federation of Women's Institutes to support approved programmes. Grants should be paid for particular types of service.

The Workers' Educational Association should give particular attention to education for the socially and culturally-deprived living in urban areas, education in industry, political and social education and courses of liberal and academic study below university level.

Consideration should be given to the establishment of a further long-term residential college in northern England.

Broadcasting organisations should develop their systematic service to education.

Educational leave
The Confederation of British Industry and the Trades Union Congress, in consultation with appropriate government departments, should be invited to take action to ensure that Britain does not lag behind other European countries in affording adequate opportunities for educational leave.

Needs

There should be more education for retirement and occupational change, broadened through a collaboration with industry and adult education agencies. Particular attention should be given to the education of women in industry.

Adult education should have a special concern for the disadvantaged – the mentally and physically handicapped and the socially disadvantaged who cannot (or will not) easily take part in normal adult education. Staff should have special training and the public should be educated about the disadvantaged.

Access to adult education

Adult education should provide opportunities for day and evening study. It should aid people transferring from one career to another. Universities should expand their part-time study facilities. The Committee of Vice-Chancellors and Principals, the Council for National Academic Awards and the Committee of Directors of Polytechnics should be invited to consider ways in which a transferable credit structure for degrees and other awards might be introduced, and with the Open University, the possibility of combined courses. Experiments with GCE courses especially for adults should be encouraged.

Finance

Students on courses at the long-term residential colleges should receive mandatory awards and the number of state scholarships for mature students should be increased.

Adult education should continue to be financed from public funds, but students should contribute to the costs. Their contributions should not be at a level which discriminated against them or against particular activities. The level should be fixed by area organisations.

Resources: accommodation and staffing

Adult education should make the maximum use of educational and community buildings at a time when they would otherwise be empty or under-used. Adult education should be combined where possible with local facilities for drama, music, art, etc. Schools serving as centres for adult education should be provided with accommodation on a scale as favourable as that provided for new schools. The Secretary of State should make it plain that public education facilities must be made jointly available to the widest possible range of users by means of skilful design management and staffing.

Staffing should be regarded as the first priority. In local education authorities, each area organisation should have a full-time professional head. Where adult education was based in a community college or further education college, adult education should be the full-time responsibility of a senior member of staff. Universities should provide for an adequate range of subject organising tutors. The Workers' Educational Association should continue to appoint organising tutors.

Salary scales for part-time staff should be adjusted swiftly and appropriately where corresponding full-time salaries are increased. Needs for training should be kept under review by the Department of Education and Science, the Development Council for Adult Education, regional advisory councils for further education, local development councils and all providing bodies.

Statistics
To counter the inadequacy of present statistics, the Department of Education and Science in consultation with the Development Council for Adult Education, the local authority associations, the Universities Council for Adult Education, the Workers' Educational Association and the National Institute for Adult Education, should review the information which should be collected and the categories to be employed.

Five-year programme of expansion
The National Institute of Adult Education and the Department should agree a five-year programme of expansion and the Department should undertake to provide sufficient grant to enable the National Institute to embark on the agreed programme.

Research
Provision should be made for research.

Action on the report

The Conservative government's White Paper, *Education: a Framework for Expansion*, published just before Russell, promised that the government would give proposals for adult education 'careful study'. But two years after publication there was still no general response to the report.

A few steps were taken by the incoming 1974 Labour government, notably the establishment of the Adult Literacy Resources Agency with £1 million a year to do some 'pump priming' to encourage local education authorities to set up local projects to help illiterates to read. With the help of the BBC, and supported by most local education authorities and a number of voluntary bodies, local projects quickly contacted about 50 000 students and the same number of volunteer teachers: a demonstration of what could be done with the right organisation and a small amount of money. The government agreed to the provision of adult state bursaries at the adult colleges and said that mature students should be eligible for mandatory awards at universities. It also made supplementary annual grants to save the Workers' Educational Association from financial disaster.

But the proposal for a development council, with the implication that it would be pushing for more money, met with no favour from a government trying to economise. After informal discussions that an advisory council, instead, would be acceptable to local authorities and adult education interests, there was a move on this front; but that was only after a critical report from the OECD examiners on the backward state of British thinking about adult education, and a powerful report published in 1976 from an Open University group, chaired by Sir Peter Venables, about the possibilities in Britain for continuing education.

In 1977, the government set up an Advisory Council for Adult and Continuing Education 'to advise generally on matters relevant to the provision of education for adults in England and Wales, and in particular to promote co-operation between the various bodies engaged in adult education, and review current practice, organisation and priorities, with a view to the most effective deployment of the available resources; and also to promote the development of future policies and priorities, with full regard to the concept of education as a process continuing throughout life.' The council was immediately invited to consider the best way of building on the adult literacy campaign, when government funding to the Adult Literacy Resources Agency ceased in 1978.

But that was clearly not the end of the Russell – or more accurately – the adult education story. The demographic tidal wave rolling through the whole education system would be receding from higher education in the mid-1980s, leaving empty places in universities and polytechnics. What was already happening in the USA suggested that higher education institutions would then start actively searching for mature students, thus opening up new opportunities for adults. There was also the European trend, stimulated by economic difficulties, towards paid educational leave, as a way of temporarily reducing and retraining the work force. It was difficult to believe that Britain could hold out against such trends. The advisory council's terms of reference seemed designed to encourage it to produce some guidelines.

A LANGUAGE FOR LIFE

report of a committee of enquiry appointed by the Secretary of State for Education and Science
1975 HMSO £5

Chairman: Sir Alan Bullock
Members: Prof. J. N. Britton, Sister B. Burbidge, Mr A. Burnet, Miss J. Derrick, Mr J. J. Fairbairn, Mr H. K. Fowler, Mr S. Froome, Mr D. Gadsby, Mr W. K. Gardner, Mr C. R. Gillings, Mrs D. M. R. Hutchcroft, Miss A. M. Johnson, Mr D. Mackay, Mr M. Marland, Prof. J. E. Merritt, Mr A. J. Puckey Mrs V. Southgate Booth, Dame Muriel Stewart, Prof. J. Wrigley.
Secretary: Mr R. Arnold, HMI.
Assistant Secretary: Mrs G. W. Dishart.

Terms of reference: To consider in relation to schools: (a) all aspects of teaching the use of English, including reading, writing, and speech; (b) how present practice might be improved and the role that initial and in-service training might play; (c) to what extent arrangements for monitoring the general level of attainment in these skills can be introduced or improved; and to make recommendations.

The major educational enquiries considered here have been set up when policy options have loomed large, or controversy bitter. Bullock came into the latter category. Public criticism of reading standards had multiplied during the early 1970s. First came the over-simplified and malicious view that Plowden advocated nothing less than a return to the Jean-Jacques Rousseau view: 'Water a child and it will grow.' Then, in 1972, came an ambiguous report on trends in reading standards from the National Foundation for Educational Research, which led many critics to believe that standards were falling. In the wake of strong criticism led by the Black Paper group of right-wing educationists, Mrs Margaret Thatcher, the Conservative Secretary of State, set up the Bullock committee.

The committee she appointed, however, had terms of reference, ranging far beyond the question of reading techniques. Bullock responded with 600 pages and over 100 recommendations, arguing that there is 'no simple nostrum for bringing out an improvement ... no substitute for a thorough understanding of the processes at work.' The report was a detailed exposition of the processes and problems of acquiring all the language skills – speech, reading and writing – at all stages, including the pre-school years and in adulthood, and the particular problems for those whose first language is not standard English. A survey of language teaching in 2000 schools provided a unique picture of what teachers actually did: the methods they used, the way they divided their time, the resources they drew on.

Bullock scattered the scaremongers without being complacent. With the Black Paper member dissenting, the committee concluded that 'the survey gives no evidence of a large body of teachers committed to the rejection of basic skills and not caring who knows it ... . It will be seen that a good deal of time is allocated to the formal practice of English ... . There appears to be little substance in the generalisations that large numbers of schools are promoting creativity at the expense of basic skills.' There was no convincing evidence that standards had fallen; though unsatisfactory tests and lack of definition on literacy did not make it easy to judge.

But that was not, said Bullock, the fundamental problem. The real issue was that 'standards are not satisfying present day requirements.' We should not be concerned with the performance of seven and nine year old children on tests which were created many years ago and the limitations of which are acknowledged, says Bullock. But it is vitally important to know whether 'the reading and writing abilities of children are adequate to the demands made upon them in school and likely to face them in adult life.' What is needed is 'functional literacy.'

Although a number of important resource recommendations were addressed to local education authorities, the greatest number of recommendations were directed to teachers. For 'if there is one general summarising conclusion we offer it is that there is nothing to equal in importance the quality and achievement of the individual teacher to whom most of our suggestions are addressed.'

Undoubtedly, one of the most significant themes in Bullock was the necessary limitation of teacher autonomy: there should be an agreed and systematic policy for each school, and standards should be externally monitored. This report marked a new stage in public concern about the curriculum, without at the same time swinging the pendulum back to recreate nineteenth century rote learning.

Main recommendations

Attitudes and standards
A system of monitoring of reading and writing should be introduced, employing new instruments, to assess a wider range of attainments than has been attempted in the past, and allowing new criteria to be established for the definition of literacy.

Responsibility for monitoring should lie with a national research organisation and 1977 should be the target date for the introduction of the new system.

The monitoring procedure should be administered between the ages of eleven and fifteen, and should be carried out by 'light sampling' methods at termly intervals to yield a rolling estimate of standards.

Organisation

There should be positive steps to develop the language ability of children in the pre-school and nursery and infant years. These should include arrangements for the involvement of parents, the improvement of staffing ratios in infant schools, and the employment of teachers' aides whose training has included a language element.

Every school should devise a systematic policy for the development of reading competence in pupils of all ages and ability levels.

Each school should have an organised policy for language across the curriculum, establishing every teacher's involvement in language and reading development throughout the years of schooling.

Every school should have a suitably qualified teacher with responsibility for advising and supporting his colleagues in language and the teaching of reading. Authorities should provide these consultant language teachers with in-service training.

There should be close consultation between schools, and the transmission of effective records, to ensure continuity in the teaching of reading and in the language development of every pupil.

English in the secondary school should have improved resources in terms of staffing, accommodation, and ancillary help.

Every local education authority should appoint a specialist English adviser and should establish an advisory team with the specific responsibility of supporting schools in all aspects: from the early years to the highest level of the secondary school.

Reading and language difficulties

Local education authorities and schools should introduce early screening procedures to prevent cumulative language and reading failure, and to guarantee individual diagnosis and treatment. A detailed profile of each child's strengths and weaknesses should accompany the child on transfer to a different school.

Additional assistance should be given to children retarded in reading, and, where it is the school's policy to withdraw pupils from their classes for special help, the children should continue to receive support at the appropriate level on their return.

There should be a reading clinic or remedial centre in every local education authority, giving access to a comprehensive diagnostic service and expert medical, psychological and teaching help. In addition to its provision for children with severe reading difficulties the centre should offer an advisory service to schools in association with the authority's specialist adviser.

Provision for the tuition of adult illiterates and semi-literates should be greatly increased, and there should be a national reference point for the co-ordination of information and support.

Local education authorities should co-ordinate the various sources of advice to adult illiterates and should provide a counselling service to introduce them to the kind of tuition best suited to their needs. The authorities should provide in-service training for tutors in adult literacy.

Children of families of overseas origin should have more substantial and sustained tuition in English. Advisers and specialist teachers are required in greater strength in areas of need.

Resources

A standing working party should be formed, made up of representatives of the Department of Education and Science and local education authorities, to consider capitation allowances and the resources of schools. This working party should as its first task recommend minimal figures for book provision, which should be kept under annual review.

Teacher education and training

A substantial course on language in education (including reading) should be part of every primary and secondary school teacher's initial training, whatever the teacher's subject or the age of the children with whom he or she will be working.

There should be an expansion of in-service education opportunities in reading, and the various other aspects of the teaching of English, and these should include courses at diploma and higher degree level. Teachers in every local education authority should have access to a language reading centre.

There should be a national centre for language in education, concerned with the teaching of English in all its aspects, from language and reading in the early years to advanced studies with sixth forms.

Action on the report

With relatively few recommendations directed at the Department of Education and Science or the local education authorities, Bullock's political impact was bound to be low-key. But in its own terms it did not do badly.

It clearly contributed to the public ferment on the curriculum, leading up to the 1977 Green Paper (see page ix). It was certainly one of the catalysts for the campaign to eradicate adult illiteracy, which was led by the British Association for Settlements and the BBC, and run between 1975 and 1978 by the Adult Literacy Resources Agency. As a result, adult literacy tutors were appointed in most local education authorities, co-ordinating voluntary teaching schemes, and, through links with public libraries, doing something to stimulate a general interest in the reading of adults and children.

The main proposals to government, on the need to monitor standards (similar to Plowden recommendations, see page 27), were taken up in part within two years of publication. Before the report it was clear that the HM Inspectorate were increasingly turning to general, publishable surveys. In 1974, units on educational disadvantage and the assessment of performance were set up within the Department of Education following a hostile report from the House of Commons Select Committee on Education, which had criticised government ignorance as to how ethnic minority children were faring. The government agreed to the national testing of pupils' performance on Bullock's 'light sampling' basis in mathematics (due to start in 1978), English (1979), science (1980) and modern languages (after 1980). Nothing however was heard of the proposal to set up a national working party on capitation allowances and the resources of schools, nor of the need for a national language centre.

Surveys in 1977 by the United Kingdom Reading Association and the University Council for the Education of Teachers suggested that there were a number of new courses with the Bullock message that 'language is for life' in colleges of education, but that some universities were blocking the relevant development of in-service courses which had no parallel in initial studies. Yet the Open University's diploma course in reading developments, taking 1 200 students a year, indicated the demand.

Inevitably, local education authority and teacher response to the report was patchy, raising the question of whether Bullock's strategy was right. Bullock is the most extreme example considered in this book of the difficulties facing those who want to promote change in the classroom. In the British decentralised system, effective processes do not exist for getting a report of this type discussed, possibly modified, and then implemented. Ironically, most of the main recommendations in Bullock needed little expenditure; for example, the recommendation for close consultation between schools and the transmission of effective records. But because the recommendations were directed at local education authorities and teachers, with no requirement to report back, it will always be difficult to measure the report's impact. The suspicion will remain that much less has been done than might have been: a sad comment on those 600 pages and 100 recommendations.

A NEW PARTNERSHIP FOR OUR SCHOOLS

report of the committee appointed jointly by the Secretary of State for Education and Science and the Secretary for Wales
1977 HMSO £3.25

Chairman: Cllr. Tom Taylor
Members: Prof. G. Baron, Miss J. Barrow, Mrs M. B. Broadley, Mr D. P. J. Browning, Cllr. E. Currie-Jones, Mrs A.E. Edwards, Mr F. D. Flower, Cllr. P. O. Fulton, Mr J. E. Hale, Mr G. M. A. Harrison, Mr R. N. Heaton, Cllr. E. G. Hett, Cllr. J. R. Horrell, Miss B. Lynn, Mr J. MacGougan, Miss A. C. Millett, Mr M. J. Moore, Rev. P. J. Reilly, Mrs J. Sallis, Mrs J. Stone, Mr K. J. Turner, Canon R. Waddington, *plus* Mr J. A. R. Kay (who resigned).
Assessors: Mr M. W. Hodges, Mr C. A. Norman, Mr S. K. Bateman, Mr J. B. Davies.
Secretary: Mr J. K. Sawtell.

Terms of reference: To review the arrangements for the management and government of maintained primary and secondary schools in England and Wales, including the composition and function of bodies of managers and governors, and their relationships with local education authorities, with head teachers and staffs of schools, with parents of pupils and with the local community at large; and to make recommendations.

Taylor, like Robbins and James, was essentially concerned with functions and powers: a brief which had generally turned out to produce the controversial reports. The committee was set up by the Labour Secretary of State, Mr Reg Prentice, to find a solution to the 1960s demand for public participation in the management of schools, which had become more strident in the tougher 1970s with a call for more effective forms of accountability.

Some of that debate is reflected in the reports considered here. Plowden, with its important findings about parental influence on their children's educational achievement, had originally suggested the need to institutionalise that interest. The reference had been taken up and strengthened by the Donnison direct grants commission and the Halsey report on the educational priority areas. Teachers began to get interested in governors as a form of worker participation or control. By the time of Bullock, the accountability tide was flowing strongly, and the Conservative party had presented itself as the champion of parents' rights. School governors were being brought into the limelight from all sorts of directions as the ideal body to reflect changing ideals about public and professional control within the educational system.

There was some reason for this. School governors had been the incarnation of the English commitment to diversity and public control. Set up under the Education Act, 1944, they were to be appointed by the local education authorities to have 'the general conduct and control of the school', including the curriculum, and a part in the appointment of the head teacher and other staff.

The theory of their position was generally stronger than the practice. For although governing bodies were to be set up for secondary schools and slightly weaker management bodies for primary schools as statutory bodies under the Education Act, Parliament did not insist that there should be separate governing bodies for each school. Some local education authorities, fearful that too much power over schools would slip out of their hands, exercised governing body powers collectively over all schools through their own education committee. The others, at any rate until the 1970s, mostly left the governing body appointments in the hands of political parties, who regarded the posts as a patronage for a narrow range of over-committed people. Either way, governing bodies tended to be ineffective, delegating most of their functions to the head teacher.

Relying more on conflict theory than on traditional concepts of hierarchical management, Taylor's proposal was disarmingly simple. Of course governing bodies should exist and should determine 'the general conduct' of the school. But they should not represent a single interest group, be it public or professional. Taylor proposed that governing bodies should be a forum in which all those with a legitimate interest could be represented, so that all those matters which were not already determined by law or local education authority policy could be argued out and settled in the one place.

It was a proposal designed to help the professionals as much as the public. All schools should have their own governing bodies to make decisions on the way the school is run because 'of the need to ensure that the school is run with as full an awareness as possible of the needs and wishes of the parents and the local community, and conversely, to ensure that these groups in their turn are better informed of the needs of the school and the policies and constraints within which the local education authority operates and the head and other teachers work.'

Main recommendations

A new approach to school government
All the powers relevant to school government should be formally vested in
the local education authority. There should be as much delegation of these
powers by the local education authority to the governing body as is
compatible with the authority's ultimate responsibility for the schools in
its area, and the governing body should grant as much discretion to the
head teacher as is compatible with the governors' responsibility for the
success of the school in all its activities.

Section 20 of the Education Act, 1944, should be repealed as soon as
possible and, from a date to be fixed by the Secretary of State, every
school should have its own separate governing body.

The term 'governing body' should be retained and applied by law to all
bodies whether they serve primary or secondary schools.

Membership of the new governing bodies
The membership of governing bodies should consist of equal numbers of
local education authority representatives, school staff (both teachers and
supporting staff), parents (with, where appropriate, pupils) and representatives of the local community. There should never be less than two members
in any one category and twenty-four should normally be regarded as the
maximum for the whole body. The head teacher of a school should always
be a member. Parent governors should be elected by parents of children
attending the school. Community representatives should be co-opted by
the governors representing the other three interest groups.

The Secretaries of State should take definitive advice on whether it is
possible to change the law to enable pupils to serve at the age of sixteen.

Communication and co-operation
With the exception of those matters which the governing body had
specifically ruled should be confidential, minutes of proceedings and
agendas should be available in the teachers' common room. The governing
body should satisfy itself that there are facilities for discussion between
members of teaching staff and for the expression of collective views.
There should be similar arrangements for supporting staff.

The governing body should be empowered to authorise the pupils to
establish a school council or similar organisation.

Parents' organisations should be encouraged, and facilities for their work
should be made available within the school.

The governing body should satisfy itself that adequate arrangements are
made to inform parents, to involve them in their children's progress and

welfare, to enlist their support and to ensure their access to the school and a teacher by reasonable arrangement.

On those occasions when the local education authority wishes to obtain local opinion on educational issues it should ensure that the consultation process draws on the knowledge and experience of the members of the newly-constituted governing bodies.

Curriculum

The governing body should be given by the local education authority the responsibility for setting the aims of the school, for considering the means by which they are pursued, for keeping under review the school's progress towards them, and for deciding upon action to facilitate such progress.

The governing body should invite the head teacher, in consultation with staff, to prepare papers setting out the means by which they propose to pursue the aims adopted.

Within the framework of any general policy made by the local education authority, the governing body should have the responsibility for formulating guidelines which promote high standards of behaviour and for making such minimum rules and sanctions as are necessary to maintain such standards in the school.

All local education authorities should review the adequacy of their advisory/inspection service in the light of the requirements proposed for the new governing bodies and should take early steps to strengthen these services as necessary, aiming at a minimum of one adviser to every 20 000 of its total population at the earliest possible date.

Every governing body should produce a first general appraisal of the school's progress, however incomplete, within four years of its formation.

Finance

Provisions corresponding to those in the 1945 model articles on submission of estimates should be applied to all schools as soon as this is practicable.

Early action should be taken by the Secretaries of State on the Bullock committee's proposal that a joint working party of representatives of the Department of Education and Science and local education authorities should be established to investigate school allowances.

Appointments

The procedure for the appointment of head teachers should provide for a small selection committee consisting equally of members of the governing body and representatives of the education committee.

The selection of deputy heads and other teachers should rest with the governing body, who should give due weight to the professional advice made available through the local education authority, to find suitable posts for teachers whose schools are closed or reorganised.

Other functions
Present arrangements for determining the responsibility for schools admissions, under which local education authorities have overall control, should continue; and the principles and criteria upon which school places are allocated should be made public.

Every local education authority should be required to make and publish procedures to be followed for the suspension of pupils.

Legislative steps should be taken to ensure that no registered pupil is debarred from school, except on medical grounds, otherwise than in compliance with the suspension procedures of the local education authority; and that no registered pupil is expelled from a school, except by the decision of the local education authority, who should inform the governing body of its decisions.

Training for new governors
All local education authorities should be required to ensure that initial and in-service training courses are available for governors. All governors should have short periods of initial training as soon as this is practicable. All governors should attend in-service training courses regularly.

Procedural arrangements
Proceedings should not be confidential unless a governing body specifically so decides, in which case any confidential items in the minutes should be recorded separately.

The local education authority should decide in the light of the local situation the most effective, practical and economic system of clerking.

Financial loss allowance should be payable to all governors in respect of proved loss of earnings. Local education authorities should be empowered to pay travelling and incidental expenses to members of governing bodies, in accordance with the normal arrangements made by authorities to secure that people are not barred from membership of a governing body by reason of the cost of attending meetings.

The government of voluntary schools
The Secretaries of State should put in hand as soon as possible consultations with representatives of the providing bodies, the local education authorities and all other parties, with a view to the adoption for voluntary schools of arrangements for management and government, following as closely as practicable the lines of those recommended for county schools.

Implementation of the recommendations

A statutory duty should be imposed on all local education authorities to make arrangements for the government of all county schools in their areas, conforming to the requirements stipulated in the report, and to publicise the arrangements.

The Secretaries of State should, within five years after this legislation comes into effect, call for reports from local education authorities on the working of the new system, and in the light of these reports issue such further guidance as may be thought desirable; and also, if need be, amend the legislation.

The Secretaries of State should arrange for progress and problems to be monitored and reported, and to be studied from an early stage by an independent agency; such as a university research group, working in close association with local education authorities and the Department of Education and Science.

Legislation should be initiated as soon as possible to give effect within five years to the requirement on local education authorities to make arrangements for individual governing bodies; and to repeal immediately section 20 of the 1944 Act, allowing for grouped governing bodies, and those sections relating to suspension and expulsion of pupils.

Action on the report

Partnership is a difficult concept for those who are used to exercising power. Although initial evidence to the committee had suggested that if governing bodies did not exist they would have had to be invented, Taylor's interpretation was immediately classified as the busybodies' charter or the administrator's nightmare by some sections of teacher and education officer opinion.

The Secretary of State, Mrs Shirley Williams, anxious to get some immediate action, wrote to the organisations representing the local education authorities, teachers, parents and local community groups, suggesting that it would be 'possible and desirable' to reach decisions about the future membership of governing bodies and the method of appointment, without commitment to the committee's recommendations on the delegation of powers to governing bodies. She indicated that she would like to see parents and teachers given better representation. But the question of the governing body's function would need 'detailed and extensive' consultations before decisions could be made.

The Secretary of State's separation of the issues of membership and power may have been designed to diffuse the controversy. But at the same time they cut the ground from under the only good argument for change:

governors should only be reformed if there was a job for them to do, and a job that they could do better than any other body.